God is
Still Speaking

God is Still Speaking

Sparking a Strategic Prayer Revival
throughout the Church

Brian Mills

Sovereign World

Sovereign World Ltd
PO Box 784
Ellel
Lancaster LA1 9DA
England

www.sovereignworld.com

ISBN: 978-1-85240-510-6

Cover design by CCD
Typeset by **documen**, www.documen.co.uk
Printed in the United Kingdom

CONTENTS

Foreword

IF EVER THERE WAS A TIME for a new look at this subject, it is now, living as we do in one of the most challenging seasons in the history of our nation and of our world. We need to be reminded of the truths that Brian has learned throughout his life and ministry.

We need to learn how God speaks today as He did to the men and women of the Old and New Testaments. I was reminded of this very powerfully on a walk recently in the ruins of an English heritage site in the Cotswolds as I heard a small child shouting, "Hello... hello... hello..." The toddler was playing hide and seek with its parents. For me it was a picture of how many people live their lives feeling that God is so remote and hard to find in the busy-ness and pressures of life. The joys of spending time with Him in prayer, worship, and reading His Word get squeezed out because of a deep-rooted belief that God couldn't possibly be speaking to me in my situation.

This book, packed full of faith-filled stories of how God has spoken into Brian's personal life, and into the churches, organizations, initiatives, and nations that he and others have sought to serve, is essential reading for every Christian seeking to follow the call of Jesus on his or her life today. I count it a privilege to have been able to work with Brian over many years and to see how God has used him, and still uses him, to make Jesus center stage in all that he seeks to do.

God is still speaking because He wants to show us more of His heart and His ways so we can usher in His Kingdom on earth. The big question is, Will we make it a priority in our own lives to stop, refocus, and listen again for His call on our lives?

Jane Holloway
World Prayer Centre;
Prayer Forum of the British Isles & Ireland

Preface

*T*HROUGHOUT MY LIFE my frequent prayer has been, "Lord, I want to know you and serve you. Please make me an extension of your Being." At first I didn't really know how that would work out. But on reflection, I have seen how God has led me over the years. Every major initiative I have taken, every major adjustment that I have made in ministry, every repositioning of myself for the future has developed out of my hearing the voice of God speaking to me.

Many times those adjustments have occurred tentatively, as I have tested whether in fact I was hearing the voice of God, or whether I had merely imagined things, or dreamed things after having the wrong kind of food! Sometimes there has been a reluctance to follow through on what I sensed God had been saying – not out of disbelief or disobedience, but more out of the fear of other people. What would they think? If others didn't see the validity of what God had been saying, then, with the best will in the world, the subsequent action taken would be seen as of the flesh and not of the Spirit. I didn't want that!

Being known as a leader of prayer is not something I have been comfortable with. When Clive Calver, my colleague and boss during part of my time at the Evangelical Alliance, suggested that I take on responsibility for prayer on behalf of the Evangelical Alliance, on the completion of my role as assistant national director of Mission England, I was very reluctant. I was more comfortable with the existing position of evangelism secretary. To be known as the "prayer and revival secretary" of the EA did not appeal to me. I had seen how Christian people tended to put on pedestals those in leadership of various national initiatives, or speakers at major conventions. Nobody deserves to be put on a pedestal in relation to prayer. We are all learners.

Although I believe in the power of prayer and have seen God do some amazing things in answer to prayer, I do not regard myself as a great pray-er. In fact the struggles I have in my personal prayer life, and the challenge to set aside quality time to pray, are similar to the experience of very many people. So how could I, with those kinds of problems, lead others? I am no expert in prayer; I doubt if anyone can be said to be! And yet I was expected to become an authority on prayer and all its aspects. These were my thoughts at the beginning.

Looking back, I am utterly amazed at how God has led me. What I have learned, and the adventures God has led me into and through, could fill many books. Even the idea for this book, and the chapter headings, came from God! Isn't it awesome that the Eternal God can communicate His will to ordinary human beings on planet earth? And that He can do this simultaneously to many of His children in multiple nations of the world? Isn't it awesome that He can do this not once but frequently, not generally but in specific ways, and so get us to the right place at the right time for the performance of His will on earth?

My prayer as I write this is that God will speak through this book, and that His children will learn to walk with Him daily, learn to hear His voice in the multiple ways He speaks, and learn to put faith into action, and feet on their prayers. Hearing His voice is not difficult. It's the obedience of faith which is!

Brian Mills
St Leonards
September 2009

CHAPTER 1

LET GOD SPEAK

―――――――――≈―――――――――

*E*VERY CHRISTIAN HAS THE CAPACITY to hear the voice of God. The question is, Do we recognize the voice of God when He speaks? And if we do, then what are we going to do about what He says?

I often hear stories of God speaking to individuals around the world who previously had no knowledge of Him. Thousands of Muslims have heard God's voice or have had a dream or vision. As a result they have become believers in Jesus. Many others testify to having heard "a voice" warning them of danger, or awakening them to faith. Even those opposed to God and His children have been known to have a supernatural encounter with God that has changed their lives. Saul of Tarsus was one of these (see Acts 9:1–6).

I believe God is speaking to us, His children, all the time. Fathers naturally want to communicate with their children, at least in theory. Even from infancy, children learn to recognize the voices of their father and mother, although it takes years for them to understand and obey what they hear! If we are created in the image of God, then obviously this capacity to hear, recognize, and relate to the voice of our natural fathers and mothers comes from Him. When our faith in God is supernaturally awakened, we are born into His family and begin to receive expressions of His love for us. From that time onwards, we have the possibility of hearing the voice of God, not just once, but regularly.

To be honest, I used to be skeptical of those people who would talk about having heard God speak to them. I used to think, Who do they think they are? God is Creator of the universe. Why would He communicate with someone that is relatively unknown? I knew what it was to put them into an "other-worldly" category. I used to wonder, How on earth can they know God is speaking to them? Surely they're just using the words in a super-spiritual sense, when what they are describing is really what they're thinking! As a young believer, these were often my thoughts. But I've learned differently over the years, and I'm so glad I have.

God's ability to speak to us is not monochrome. All of creation speaks to us of His creative essence. The sheer beauty and variety of His creation, from the grandeur of lofty mountains to the minuteness of tiny insects, causes us to wonder in amazement. Romans 1:20 reminds us that the witness of creation speaks.

God speaks to us through others. Most of us can relate to this. Through sermons, books, videos, and letters, we pick up insights which enable us to grow in our understanding of the will of God for our lives. But to recognize the inner voice of God's Spirit is what Christians find most difficult.

Most of us walking down a busy street will, if our hearing is unimpaired, hear the dropping of a coin on the pavement. We recognize the sound. But it takes an entomologist to hear and recognize the unique sound of a grasshopper on the pavement! Child of God, do you recognize His voice when He speaks? Are you listening to His voice and doing what He says?

Prayer is the means for us to be able to hear God's voice. Through prayer we consciously draw near to God and have a conversation with Him. Now, my understanding of a conversation is that it is two-way! If I ask Him a question, then do I expect to get an answer? These days I have found that my prayer life is not so much a list of requests as of questions: "Lord, what do you think of all this mess we're in?" "How do I pray in this situation?" "Lord, what is this person's *real* need?" When I pray like that, I expect Him to talk back to me, or show me something I hadn't seen but which I need to see in order to pray according to His will, and from His perspective.

We don't need to be mature Christians to hear God's voice. In fact many of us are becoming amazed at the ability of young children to hear God's voice. A child of five years of age came into breakfast one morning in the home of her grandmother, an Irish prayer leader with whom I was staying.

"Jesus is coming soon," said the little girl. "It's time to get ready. There's much work to be done. Jesus is coming soon."

"Have you been talking with her about Jesus coming back?" I asked.

"No," said her grandmother, "but this is the second time this week she's told us that."

For many years I have wanted to write a book on guidance. How do we know what God's will is in any given situation? Does He guide us only about the important decisions in life or about the specific things of everyday life as well? As a very young Christian I devoured books on guidance, because I genuinely wanted to do the will of God. Usually there was a methodology about the principles of guidance portrayed. It went something like this:

1. You need the inner witness of God's Spirit. Do you feel you are being led in a particular direction? (Usually this

was interpreted as being inwardly comfortable about the anticipated course of action.)

2. You need the upward witness of the Word of God. What scriptures has God been leading you to?

3. You need the outward witness of others. What is the advice being given by your elders and friends?

4. You need the witness of circumstances. What significant events are occurring to point you in a certain direction?

Although some find it helpful to have these pointers for guidance in some of the big questions of life – such as career, marriage partner, where to live – nevertheless hearing the voice of God is not limited to either these issues or these mechanisms. He can speak to us about anything, anyone, and anywhere. God is not limited by our methodologies or time constraints. Much of the way He guides us is beyond blueprints.

Three years after taking up my first post in so-called "full-time ministry," both my wife and I felt that it was time to move on and that God wanted us to leave the mission for which I had been assistant secretary. It was 31 December, my last day in the employ of Central Asian Mission, a faith mission which is now defunct. We had been asking God in prayer, "What next?" As I would be unemployed on 1 January and had a wife and two small children to provide for, I naturally felt responsible for my family. Not to provide for one's own would label me worse than an unbeliever (1 Timothy 5:8)! So, during my lunch break, I determined to visit an employment agency to find a temporary job until God showed us more specifically what we were to do.

As I walked into this agency, the voice of God said to me, "You've asked me to guide you – why won't you trust me?" It wasn't the audible voice of God, but it could just as well have been! I was stopped in my tracks. I turned around, walked into a nearby doorway, and stood for a few minutes in silent prayer, talking it over with God. An hour later I was visiting another Christian office to use their tape-recording facilities to finish an audio-visual presentation I had been working on. Before I left that office, I was interviewed by their general secretary and appointed to help in their office, starting at 9 a.m. the next morning! None of this was in prospect at the start of the day.

As I arrived home later that day, my wife greeted me with, "You've got a job!"

"How do you know?" I asked.

"I was praying this afternoon, and God told me you would come home with a job."

So started nine months of happy relationship with SASRA (The Soldiers' and Airmen's Scripture Readers Association) where my skills were used, and through whom God provided for us as a family, even though we and they knew this was going to be a temporary arrangement.

If our relationship with God is not active, or is spasmodic, our ability to hear God speaking to us may be limited. But if God can communicate with any of us, as He did with us as a young married couple, then isn't that relationship with Him worth pursuing?

Christians, young in faith, may need to hear the voice of God in order for them to be kept on the right track. Some of my friends over the years have implied that when we are young in the faith we all need to hear God's voice clearly, but as we grow in our knowledge of God the hearing of His voice is not so necessary. Is this really true? Older Christians certainly should be more mature in their faith. Does that "maturity" imply that we should be making up our own mind as to what is "good to the Holy Spirit and to us"? Or is that merely a human response made by well-meaning Christians who, plagued by busy lifestyles, have for long years settled for not hearing the voice of God?

On the other hand, I hear other well-meaning Christians suggest that children can't be expected to hear God's voice. Really? Why not? If they do, it is suggested, we should be wary, since "everyone knows that children have fertile imaginations." Does that prevent God from speaking to them? I believe all Christians, whatever their age or maturity, whether or not they have fertile imaginations, should be able clearly to hear God's voice throughout their lives!

It is possible that most, if not all, of us as God's children do hear Him speaking regularly. The question is, What do we do about what He says? Some ignore it, because it may be uncomfortable to hear, or because we are not sure if we really are hearing His voice. Perhaps, even for us adults, we may think it is our imagination playing tricks. So, we deliberately edit out God's voice. We all know what it is like not to pay attention to someone who is speaking to us. Eventually that person will cease speaking to us. Unlike other people, however, God still wants to get through to us.

> Those who are led by the Spirit of God are sons of God … The Spirit himself testifies with our spirit that we are God's children.
>
> (Romans 8:14, 16)

In Scripture, God spoke directly to prophets, priests, kings, and the disciples, as well as to Jesus. Sometimes He spoke His word to those with whom there was no relationship, such as Nebuchadnezzar, king of the Babylonians (see Daniel chapters 2 and 4). He even used an ass through which to speak His word! He is not confined to people's previous understandings. He is not even confinable!

God spoke through dreams, visions, prophetic words of knowledge, and words of wisdom. He spoke through angels and through the inner voice of His Spirit. Sometimes His voice was like thunder (2 Samuel 22:14); at other times it was a whisper (1 Kings 19:12). The Greek word for "voice" is "phone." So the little boy got it right when he sang, *"God is still on the phone"* (whereas he should have sung, *"God is still on the throne"*)! He is still speaking – are we listening?

Hearing God's voice seems to be the most obvious evidence of the relationship between human beings – creatures created in God's image – and God Himself. Most of the writings of the major and minor prophets consist of the words spoken to them by God. At times, of course, the historical context is described, because God does not speak in a vacuum; He speaks to and into real-life situations. What we get in Scripture are the words that God speaks to nations and, more particularly, to His people. The time is located for us in relation to the reign of particular kings. God is concerned with how nations are led and He still is today. So where are the prophets who can speak to nations? Fortunately they are here. God has given to many of His servants today the opportunity to speak to and with leaders of governments and nations. Some of those in power actually want to know, "Is there a word from God?"

Rarely do we find recorded in Scripture the words that God spoke to His servants personally, about themselves, their character, and their day-to-day living. But I expect they heard God speak to them about that as well; so that, whenever He spoke the significant words that created change, they were able to detect those words as the voice of God. He did not even speak to *them* in a vacuum, but against the background of their relationship with Him. Isn't it interesting that when God initially spoke to Moses, Gideon, and Jeremiah, their response was to look at themselves and their limitations? Moses was afraid and said,

Who am I?

(Exodus 3:11)

Gideon said,

> My clan is the weakest in Manasseh, and I am the least in
> my family.
>
> (Judges 6:15)

And Jeremiah said,

> I do not know how to speak; I am only a child.
>
> (Jeremiah 1:6)

God doesn't deal with us according to our suitability, nor does
He wait for us to achieve a certain level of understanding.

When Adam and Eve were shut out of the Garden of
Eden, they were excluded from the presence of God. Their
fellowship was curtailed because of their sin – that of listening to another voice, the voice of a serpent! But God's
chosen vessels continued to be able to hear His voice at
times, and certainly had the possibility of renewed fellowship. Otherwise, how was it that Enoch was able to walk
with God? Abraham, Moses, Joshua, Joseph, Samuel, David,
and many others enjoyed fellowship with God, as well as
being the channels through whom His word was delivered
and His will was done, despite their own limitations.

When God spoke to His servants, they mostly didn't
need to check out the validity of what they were hearing
for approval. They were messengers for God. So when
Micaiah prophesied, he spoke only what God had told him
to say (see 2 Chronicles 18:13). But in passing on God's
words to Ahab and Jehoshaphat, he was ridiculed and
physically assaulted (2 Chronicles 18:23–27). We are not
responsible for people's reactions to God's word, but we
are responsible for both the timing and the way in which
we deliver His word. That's where the advice of others
may be helpful.

Have you ever noticed how many times in Paul's experience he heard the voice of God, and received fresh instructions for the future? He didn't receive redirections for his missionary journeys from a committee, but from God. As a new believer, fresh from an extraordinary manifestation of the risen Lord in blinding light on his way to Damascus, Saul (as he was then) is found in prayer in a house on Straight Street. There he has a vision of a man named Ananias coming to pray and lay hands on him to bring back his sight (Acts 9:10–19). Not only did his sight return, but through Ananias' obedience, against his own prejudice, Saul is introduced to the Christian community in Damascus – the very community he had intended to capture and imprison.

Have you also noticed that God communicated with Paul during the night? At Troas he has his vision of a man from Macedonia begging him, "Come over to Macedonia to help us" (Acts 16:9). At Corinth Paul faced persecution and opposition from the Jews. But God was at work, bringing many Greeks into faith. One night the Lord again spoke to Paul in a vision:

> Do not be afraid; keep on speaking, do not be silent.
>
> (Acts 18:9)

So he stayed there for eighteen months, teaching the Word of God. This was a new departure for Paul, who up until then had been an itinerant preacher.

Once, during prayer, Paul was in a trance (or "overwhelmed" – the Greek word means to be in an "ecstasy") during which God spoke to him. We don't know whether he was asleep naturally or "out in the Spirit" supernaturally. What really mattered was that he heard God speak to him yet again:

> Quick! … Leave Jerusalem immediately … I will send you far away to the Gentiles. (Acts 22:17–21)

Paul's life is in danger once more, but this time he is not to stay and preach it out, but to go. God doesn't want us to rely on yesterday's experience for today's challenges and tomorrow's opportunities. He wants to keep on speaking fresh things into our lives.

Paul is back in Jerusalem. He had caused uproar as he testified before the Jewish Sanhedrin. The Pharisees and Sadducees had fallen out, and Paul had ended up being rescued by the military. It is night-time again. This time the Lord stands near Paul:

> Take courage! As you have testified about me in Jerusalem, so you must also testify in Rome.
>
> (Acts 23:11)

A plot to kill Paul is discovered, and for his own safety he is removed to Caesarea – the first stage of his journey to Rome. When a Mediterranean storm threatens to end all that, God again speaks to him, this time through an angel:

> Do not be afraid, Paul. You must stand trial before Caesar [the most powerful man in the world at that time]; and God has graciously given you the lives of all who sail with you.
>
> (Acts 27:22–25)

With God, Paul and those traveling with him were as safe as houses!

And so Paul's preaching in centers of learning within Greece caused the gospel to influence Greek thought, and to be transmitted through the Greek language. His journey to Rome caused the gospel to be gossiped from morning to evening every day for two years to small and great alike (Acts 28:23, 30). His message was simple. He preached the Kingdom of God and taught about Jesus. He told them that this message wasn't just for them; it was also for the

Gentiles – "and they will listen!" (Acts 28:28–31). As a result it was then taken to the far-flung reaches of the Roman Empire, including ancient Britain. Where would we be today if Paul had chosen to ignore the voice of God, or edit out what he heard God say because it was inconvenient, or allowed his natural fear of danger and of the authorities to overwhelm him?

And yet today, many Gentile Christians, having heard God speak, choose to ignore God's word, or they allow themselves to be hoodwinked by the suggestion that it might be their imagination. Or else the fear of what others may say, think, or do lulls them into a passive kind of disobedience. Must it be only the prophets, the initiators of specialist ministries, and missionaries who hear the voice of God?

If hearing the voice of God is the most obvious evidence of human beings' relationship with Him (according to Scripture), why is there so little evidence of us being encouraged to seek that kind of fellowship with God today? Are we listening to too many other voices, and not enough for and to the voice of God? We listen to the voice of the media, to politicians, to experts in various fields, to educators. We listen also to the voice of temptation in its various forms. We hear the voices of our detractors. We listen to the insinuations and accusations of the enemy of our souls, either in our minds or in the voices of others. We listen to carping criticism, even that of our brothers and sisters, sometimes forgetting that in so doing we give ear to the one who is the Accuser and who seeks to lead the whole world astray (Revelation 12:9–10). But where are those who will listen primarily for what God says?

God is calling His Church and His children to listen to His voice and take notice of what He says. Christians – young or old, male or female, experienced or newborn – God can speak to you, wants to speak to and with you,

and will speak to you. Will you listen? What He says may
not only influence what you do in the future, but may also
influence the ends of the earth. God can work through any
one of us who is prepared to take Him seriously, walk with
Him in humility and obedience, and do what He asks.

Those with a more public prophetic ministry need
constantly to hear God's voice too. The prophet Amos said:

> Surely the Sovereign LORD does nothing
> > without revealing his plan
> > to his servants the prophets.
> The lion has roared –
> > who will not fear?
> The Sovereign LORD has spoken –
> > who can but prophesy?
>
> (Amos 3:7–8)

And Moses said,

> I wish that all the LORD's people were prophets!
> (Numbers 11:29)

Prophetic utterances and understanding need not be seen as
the prerogative of the few, but the practice of the many.

Go back to God. Ask Him to renew your relationship
with Him and to lead you into His paths, whatever the cost.
Be in His presence. Start asking Him to speak to and with
you, as well as through you. And don't be surprised if He
answers! At first it may just be about your character and
your relationship with Him. Soak it up. Get used to hearing
His voice as a normal part of your walk in the Spirit. Then,
maybe, God will use you to speak His word to others, or to
apply His word through powerful intercession.

CHAPTER 2

A JOURNEY IN PRAYER

———————— ≈ ————————

GOD HAS LED ME on a remarkable journey. I was an ordinary Christian, working in a bank, when God started to speak to me about serving Him in a so-called "full-time" capacity. Initially He used circumstances (the stillbirth of our first child) and the counsel of older, wiser Christians to get our attention. Then He started to incline our hearts towards full-time ministry with the Central Asian Mission. During three years of what I now see as an apprenticeship as the assistant secretary of the Central Asian Mission, and as its youth secretary, God led me to form a youth prayer movement called The Mountaineers. Through this, we were focusing prayer on the mountain regions of Central Asia, in which the highest mountain, Everest, had recently been successfully climbed for the first time.

It is ironic that one of the first initiatives God had me take was to form a youth prayer movement, when at the time prayer was not a priority in my life! Through it, in quite a remarkable way, Roger Mitchell and I became connected. He was one of the first young men to enroll in this youth prayer movement, even though we didn't know each other at the time!

Because of this connection with Central Asia, my wife, Ruth, and I expected God would lead us to go and serve Him in the region. Several missionary agencies approached us with specific roles and responsibilities in mind. We were very open to going, but God stopped us in our tracks. God spoke to us through Isaiah 33:19–21:

> You will see ... no more,
> > those people of an obscure speech,
> > with their strange, incomprehensible tongue ...
> your eyes will see Jerusalem,
> > a peaceful abode, a tent that will not be moved;
> its stakes will never be pulled up ...
> There the LORD will be our Mighty One.
> > It will be like a place of broad rivers and streams ...
> > no mighty ship will sail them.

Within a year, we were leading a Brethren-based evangelistic mission called Counties, with twenty evangelists operating in tents in southern England – our Jerusalem! And we had to move to live in an area of Surrey where there were rivers and streams that "no mighty ship" would go on. God is very specific! We would never have chosen a denominational agency, since our sympathies had always been with Christians of all denominations and none. But God had different ideas.

So started fourteen years of fruitful service in a ministry that became one of the largest evangelistic agencies in Britain, producing some well-known evangelists. And so developed for me a focus on reaping the spiritual harvest, which has proved foundational to everything into which God has subsequently led us.

But still prayer was not a priority! Oh, yes, we prayed. We had prayer meetings for the missions. Sometimes, when things did not go well, we had extended times of prayer. When we did, we invariably began to experience something supernatural. One of the evangelists was affectionately referred to as "I've-a-praying-pal" – his name was Ivor Powell! He was always praying, and had in his spirit a longing and expectation for revival. He used to tell me of the way in which God had given him that expectation – and when he did so, his eyes lit up. We knew he had touched something divine. As a result he wanted to live close to God, and wanted the rest of us to do the same.

When prayer is seen as the last resort – when it is merely a response to a crisis – then it represents an inadequate understanding of prayer. Prayer is more than that. But it took me many years before I began to experience this for myself.

Early on, I recognized that prayer was a key element in every historic revival. I used to read any book I could find about revival (or "spiritual awakening," as Americans understand it). Every revival in history has been preceded by, and accompanied by, what is known as "extraordinary prayer." Revival is born in prayer and continues just as long as revival prayer continues. But one can read the stories of revival and learn about prayer through the experience of others, without it affecting oneself. It was like that with me – until 1978.

During that year I had an experience of the Holy Spirit which proved to be life-changing, one of the results of which was a deeper relationship with God. The charismatic or renewal movement was already an accepted part of church life. People positioned themselves as either for or against it. I was very happy to fellowship with those who had some kind of powerful experience of God, as I was with those who hadn't. I wanted to be open to every type of Christian. But I didn't have to become like those branded as "charismatics," or accept all their theological foibles. Then God did something in me.

One of my colleagues, John Sparkes, telephoned me to tell of a remarkable Sunday communion service at his recently planted church in Suffolk. The Holy Spirit had moved in and among the congregation so that everyone was on their faces before God, and the service lasted well beyond its allotted time. People began to be overwhelmed by the Holy Spirit; some spoke in other tongues. Two weeks later I visited John to find out more. I met many of the Christians in his fellowship. Some I had known for a while; others were quite young in the faith. But something remarkable had happened. They had fallen in love with the Lord and couldn't stop speaking about their relationship with Him. These newer Christians were now streets ahead of me in their knowledge and experience of God. They had an intimacy with God that I knew was lacking in my life.

On my second day with the Sparkes family, I asked to be excused from breakfast and from their company. I went off to seek God on my own. For hours I prayed and sought His face on a Suffolk beach, between Thorpeness and Sizewell. I was taken on a kind of expedition around Scripture by God's Spirit; all of the Biblical references had to do with knowing God for Himself. I began to realize that, up until then, I was reading Scripture in order to get sermons, rather than to feed on God and His Word. Later that day I arrived at the home of another evangelist colleague to stay the night. He asked if I would be a babysitter, since he and his wife wished to go to a late-night birthday party for a friend. I was delighted. It enabled me to be alone with God. So, until the early hours of the morning, I was in His presence, weeping, listening, reading His Word. For many days this happened. Existing on four hours' sleep per night, the rest of the twenty-four hours was a time when God began to draw me closer and closer towards Him. Car journeys and walks all became occasions to fellowship with God. I was experiencing His love in a new, powerful way. God was teaching me that prayer principally and primarily was about relationship with Him.

Just over a year later, my wife Ruth joined in a joint church event in our home town of Wokingham to put on a musical called *Spirit*. Over many weeks there were rehearsals for musicians, choirs, drama groups, dancers, and many other artistic contributors. Recognizing the spiritual significance of what they were doing, some of the leaders formed a prayer group to pray through the difficulties and for the churches to experience something of the overflow. For many weeks, with Ruth doing rehearsals and meeting for prayer, and me traveling around in ministry, the two of us seemed to pass like ships in the night!

Two weeks before the musical was due to be presented, she invited me to go with her to the prayer meeting. I readily agreed – for the sole reason of being with my wife for an evening! Nearly all those at the prayer meeting were unknown to me. They were from Anglican, Methodist, Roman Catholic, Brethren, and other free-church backgrounds. The two hours of prayer together were wonderful. Then, at the end, the leader announced, "Next week will be our last prayer meeting. After that, we'll be presenting the musical."

"You can't stop this prayer meeting!" I chimed in. "This is the most wonderful prayer meeting I've ever been in. Something special is happening among you and through you."

Fortunately the rest agreed with me. So, after the week of musical presentations, we continued with our prayer meetings. There were about fifteen of us. We prayed for each other, for our families, for our churches and for our town. For two hours each Monday evening we met. The words of the *Spirit* musical (and of Scripture) often punctuated the prayer times. We opened up ourselves to what the Spirit might want to do in, with, and through us, as the early disciples had also done.

For fifteen months we met weekly. They were wonderful times of prayer. We grew very close as a group – so much so that even now, more than twenty-five years later, the members of that group remain among our closest friends, even though we are scattered across the United Kingdom (and elsewhere in the world). We grew in our relationship with God and with one another.

Others in our churches began to hear about what God was doing among us, and started asking if they could join us. So, about a year later, we decided to open the prayer time to invite others in. Soon there was a pool of some fifty people coming. We had to split the group into three, and then add another night of the week into our schedule to allow the original core group to continue to pray with each other. We wanted to continue to move on in our knowledge and experience of prayer and of God, and not be restrained by the developing understanding of some of the newer ones in the group.

Then, as I was about to join the Evangelical Alliance of Great Britain and Northern Ireland as evangelism secretary, one of our group suggested, "Why don't we men meet early every morning for a week to pray for you, Brian?"

"How early?" I asked. We agreed to meet at 6 a.m., mainly because one of our group came off night shifts then. I thought I could probably manage a week of early morning prayer meetings, even though early rising was certainly not my strong point! We continued that early morning tryst for nearly two years. God was so good. He answered many of our prayers. People around the country began to hear about the Wokingham prayer group and sent in prayer requests. One month, we kept a record of 120 specific requests, and the answers to those prayers.

So, within our town, we had prayer groups two evenings weekly, morning prayer every day, a monthly day of prayer and fasting, and a monthly "Praise and Prayer" gathering in the local town hall. For all of us, this time was the most fruitful and meaningful in the whole of our lives. The prayer meeting became our laboratory. This was where we were learning more about God and about prayer.

Soon after joining the Evangelical Alliance, I became part of the national team responsible for setting up and leading Mission England (a three-year period of corporate preparation for mission, involving the Church throughout the nation and culminating in a three-month period of evangelistic missions with Dr Billy Graham, held in football stadia). My initial role in it was to get the Church throughout England (and indeed the world) praying. The experiences God was giving us in Wokingham became the context out of which flowed everything else I was to do throughout that period. However, it was one thing to be involved in prayer in a small town; it was quite another thing to organize prayer throughout the nation, as I was about to learn.

All that God was teaching us in Wokingham about Himself, about small-group prayer, about praying across denominational barriers, about being specific in prayer, about sacrificial prayer – all this and more became foundational to every initiative that God eventually led me to take.

We learned about how to lead small prayer groups. God taught us the difference between intercession and prayer. Unity of heart and mind, as well as cross-denominational unity, became essential. Confession of one's faults to one another and praying for one another became important for effective prayer (see James 5:16). Each week, as we gathered, we would instinctively be aware if things weren't right in any of our lives or in our marriages or family life. Instead of hiding this, we opened up to one another and prayed things through. As we shared the problem or pain – in a safe and trusting environment – we would pray. In this way we kept no secrets and didn't mind making ourselves vulnerable, because we were seeing, as a result of our prayers, the power of God at work and, more importantly, the power of His love.

We learned the importance of moving blockages and discerning why prayer seemed not to be answered in certain situations. If we weren't seeing God break through in situations about which we were praying, we would ask God to reveal to us what we were missing. God led us to appreciate the reality of the demonic, and He led some of us into deliverance ministry. He led us also into healing ministry, both of the physical and the emotional. We learned to listen to the Lord for His keys to unlock difficult situations. Having "words of knowledge" for people became the source of wonderful discoveries. We found out that God could speak through dreams or wake us up in the middle of the night. Praying the word of God into situations became part of how we functioned. God loved the people we were praying for and, through His insights, we were learning to see that what *He* knew was more important than what *we* knew!

For all of us, this was new territory. The Holy Spirit was our Guide as well as the Comforter. We didn't learn from manuals, although since then manuals have been written for others! We didn't learn from books, although books on prayer have been written – both before and since then! We didn't even learn from others with more experience than ourselves, because at the time we were unaware of others to whom God was saying similar things. However, we have learned of much more since!

The thing that strikes me about that time is that we were all novices. We were like little children discovering a whole new world out of our relationship with our Dad in Heaven. We had no pretensions about our importance. We were ordinary people from ordinary churches, learning about an extraordinary God. So the rest of this book is about how God leads, how He speaks, and what happens when we obey. This is not about me, or us as a married couple, or us as a prayer group. People feature in it, of course.

But this is principally about a wonder-working God and the way in which, through His interaction with His children, He can cause His will to be done on earth as it is in heaven. It is about what happens when God speaks, and His people listen and do what He says.

CHAPTER 3

PRAYER TRIPLETS AND CELLS
FOR GROWTH

YEARS AGO I HEARD OF A MAN who had a book in which he wrote the names of all the people he prayed for. Quietly, throughout his life, he would write down the names. At the end of his life, when his possessions were being sorted through, eighteen books were found, in which were over 2,400 names. Against each name were two dates. The first date was the day on which he started to pray, and the second date was the day the person was converted.

I admire the perseverance and the prayer life of someone like that. I only wish I was like that, and even more, that all of God's children could be like that. How the Church would grow!

Such stories not only inspire me, but also provide me with the challenge to make it happen. Before the formal start of Mission England (1982–85), the national team consisting of Gavin Reid, Eddie Gibbs, Clive Calver, and me, together with our chairman Tom Houston, met together frequently. It was a time for dreaming dreams, envisioning one another, making plans, and taking initiatives. We had embarked on the early stages of a national mission to touch every sector of society and every city, town, and village in England. We all had experience in leading national movements and were committed to evangelism. We had been part of a working group of leaders at national level that had published a report, "Let My People Grow," which had gained widespread exposure in all branches of the Church. We were learning about church growth principles from elsewhere in the world and from missiologists. If there was to be any growth in the Church in England, there needed to be a fundamental change in existing attitudes. We had to embark on a period of training and envisioning, which could culminate in an extensive period of mission in multiple centers around England.

Our idea was to have two years of training and one year of outreach, with subsequent years of follow-up and consolidation. Through the help of agencies like the Bible Society, Scripture Union, and the Church Pastoral Aid Society, we were able to publish the training courses that we compiled between us. Gavin Reid and Eddie Gibbs were particularly skilled at this and took the major responsibility, although we each had input into the material. We set up courses around the country in which we trained trainers, so that within their regions they could be available to provide training in the churches.

Before all this could occur, we recognized we had to do an envisioning tour around the country to bring Christians together and to alert the Church to our vision and plans. Clive Calver, then the director of British Youth for Christ, had a good deal of experience in arranging tours through his YFC connections, so he took responsibility for putting on a series of events called Prepare the Way. Then the team turned to me and said, "Brian, you are the person to get the Church in the nation praying." I didn't baulk at this. I was the only one at the time, I think, that was actively involved in prayer groups across the denominational spectrum. (This was the period described in the previous chapter.)

But how was I to go about motivating the Church to pray? At the time there were few prayer movements in existence. I knew only about Intercessors for Britain and the Lydia Fellowship. Evelyn Christenson, the American author of books on prayer, had done a tour among women, from which a small new movement, Prayer Chain Ministry, had begun in Scotland and Northern Ireland. Dick Eastman, another American mission leader, had introduced his Change the World School of Prayer at several locations. But at the time there was no existing prayer organization to follow up on this. Crusade for World Revival, producers of *Every Day with Jesus* and *Revival* magazine, had a strong prayer emphasis within their publications. But that was about it!

At first I had no idea how to go about things. I asked God to guide me and give me the key to mobilizing the Church in the nation to pray. One day a Christian from Guildford telephoned my office asking to see me as he had something to share with me. My secretary tried to put him off as she knew I was very busy trying to do many things, as usual! Nevertheless he was insistent. So eventually he came to my home.

"God has told me that you are struggling to find a key," he said, "and that others are asking you to come up with a plan. You are not to be pressured into things. God wants you to wait before Him until He shows you the key." He could not have known about my responsibility to get the Church in the nation praying. Nor could he have known that my colleagues were pressurizing me to come up with a plan. I took his word as from God. And I waited.

A few weeks later, I was having a bath, reflecting on a mini-tour I had just completed with Steve Maxted, during which he had talked about small-group prayer. As I pondered this, I found myself thinking in threes. If we could get people meeting together in threes to pray for their friends by name – three each – so that between them the group of three became committed to pray regularly for nine altogether, then this might work, I thought. I had already discovered that God is at work in our thoughts if we are walking with Him. This was such an occasion. God was speaking to me through my thoughts.

As one does, I had a discussion with God in the bath. I asked Him about the idea. The Holy Spirit was leading to me to think of threes meeting together in neighborhoods, colleges, schools, and businesses, praying for those they had most contact with who were not Christians. Praying together in threes meant that they could encourage one another by praying for each other's friends, as well as their own. They could be praying for each other when they knew that something positive and active was going on. This would be an active, regular, weekly commitment.

And so the idea concerning small-group prayer was shared with the rest of the team. It was Gavin Reid who coined the phrase "prayer triplets." The vision was launched through the Prepare the Way tour that was held in multiple venues throughout England. This tour kick-started the Mission England program of church growth and evangelism. Before long, prayer triplets were multiplying all over England. Within weeks we were beginning to hear of people becoming Christians. Some groups were seeing five or six of the prayed-for people converted in as many weeks. Scripture Union helped by producing materials targeted at school and college Christians. Groups were starting in many walks of life. Maxi-groups (three married couples) as well as mini-groups (three individuals) were being formed. This vision for prayer caught on so quickly that we weren't equipped to maintain contact or monitor what was going on. God took it and multiplied it. He gave us the key, we sowed the seed, and the rest was the work of the Holy Spirit.

There was a need for some teaching on prayer, so I arranged a series of seminars throughout the country. We had to devise some teaching materials to help people understand some of the dynamics at work as we pray. Evelyn Christenson returned for another tour, which I helped to set up. I joined her at every venue. In six cities a total of 12,000 women had a day's teaching on prayer and were introduced to prayer triplets. Evelyn was so impressed that she took the materials and started to speak about prayer triplets wherever she went in the world. Within six months, we were hearing of prayer triplets being started on every continent. There were even prayer triplets in the palace of the king of Tonga!

We asked for regional prayer coordinators to be appointed. Each of them took the vision and worked at multiplying it within their region. As each region was establishing church-based coordinators as well, these regional prayer coordinators then arranged some gatherings to equip church-based leaders. Within every training event during that year of 1983, prayer triplets were launched. By the beginning of 1984 we began to ask those attending preparation meetings how many were in prayer triplets, and how many of the groups had seen at least one person converted. From all the feedback we had, we estimated that something like 30,000 prayer triplet groups existed, and that 12 percent of them had seen at least one person converted. Most of us had also met many individuals who had seen all nine of the people their group was praying for brought to Christ. Factoring this in, we conservatively estimated that 4,000 new Christians were in the Kingdom of God and within our churches as a result of prayer – many weeks before Billy Graham arrived. This was exciting and new. A few churches even doubled in size through the answers to prayers offered in their prayer triplet groups.

When the evangelistic phase of the mission took place, the response to the preaching of Billy Graham was twice the expectation, and the percentage response was double what he had experienced elsewhere in his long and distinguished ministry. Most observers considered that the reason for this fruit was due to the success of prayer triplets.

A fuller story of what God did at that time has been written in *Three Times Three Equals Twelve: God's Strategy for Church Growth through Prayer Triplets.*[1] This book was also published in Australia as the recommended Christian book for the bicentennial anniversary of Australia's founding, under the title *Prayer Triplets*. But the story didn't end with Mission England, nor with the evangelistic phase.

Since then, many British evangelists began to include prayer triplets as part of their preparation for missions throughout the late 1980s and 1990s. I was involved frequently in doing prayer preparation teaching for Eric Delve, the Saltmine Team, J. John, and Don Double. Mission Wales with Luis Palau included prayer triplets. Billy Graham returned for further stadium meetings in Sheffield in 1985 and in London in 1989. At the same time some 600 video missions were held throughout the British Isles. All of these also included prayer triplets as part of their preparation.

Students going up to universities were encouraged in their first term to form prayer triplets on the corridors of their halls of residence, as a means of providing a caring context for their own spiritual safety, as well as enabling them to reach out to others. Through the Evangelical Alliance we produced over the years a variety of materials for use by churches to encourage bringing mission triplets and community triplets into being. At large-scale events, like Explo 85, prayer triplets were introduced to the many thousands of young people attending the locations throughout Europe. Prayer triplets were transforming the experience of Christians in many nations, leading to large numbers coming to Christ. I've heard of programs based on prayer triplets being launched nationwide in Switzerland, Sri Lanka, Zimbabwe, Australia, and India. The Billy Graham Evangelistic Association adapted the vision for use in their ongoing ministry and missions.

The original intention within our Mission England strategy was for prayer triplets to continue beyond the mission phase. We envisaged that triplets would have a life of twelve to eighteen months anyway. After that, they needed to split so as to involve the new converts in good prayer habits and to bring in Christians who had not been involved before. In this way, the growth being experienced in the early days could continue. Unfortunately, most saw it as a tool for prayer-evangelism, which then tended to be discontinued after the evangelistic phase. Why? Because the momentum was not continued, the vision and motivation was not there. Unfortunately, in Britain we tend to see prayer and evangelism as events rather than as processes. To this day it is a cause for personal regret that we didn't mount an ongoing national strategy to encourage an ongoing prayer triplet movement. I think we could have seen much more blessing had we done so.

In the late 1990s prayer triplets turned up in another form. The burgeoning cell-church movement has included prayer triplets as their main means of growth. The process known as "G12" is an exact application of the idea. Three people meet together to pray for nine others. When all nine are converted, they are incorporated with the group of three to form a cell. After a period of growing together, the twelve then split off to form four more triplet groups and repeat the process.

Mathias Bolsterli, leader of the International Christian Fellowship in Zurich, was told by God that he had to postpone a planned holiday with his family and instead accompany me on a tour of Swiss cities. I had been invited to launch prayer triplets and a new publication about prayer that I had authored (translated into Swiss German). He understood from God that he was going to learn something that would be vital for his future ministry. I had not met Mathias before, so to hear this at our first meeting was a bit overwhelming! But I had to trust God that He would implant something. Mathias came as my translator, and so night after night he heard about prayer and more specifically about prayer triplets. He had recently started a cell church.

After the tour he began to introduce prayer triplets into the church's cell structure. Each week, each of the cells was to break down into prayer triplets at some stage during the evening and pray for their non-Christian friends. Once a month each cell planned a social event to which they invited their prayed-for friends. From this, people were attracted into other "sinner-friendly" activities of the church, which included a regular Sunday evening multi-media presentation of the gospel. The church he started has since then extended into many other cities within Europe, each having a similar "DNA." The Zurich church, meanwhile, has grown to be the largest in Switzerland. It is a praying church!

So did this simple "idea" get born in a bath? Not really. It was part of God's DNA for His children long before. Jesus speaks about the power of agreement in prayer:

> If two of you on earth agree about anything you ask for, it will be done for you by my Father in heaven. For where two or three come together in my name, there am I with them.
>
> (Matthew 18:19–20)

Groups all over the world have found this to be true. This is more than a proof text for small numbers. Jesus never uses words wastefully. There is a dynamic in the numbers He used. He had his own prayer triplet: Peter, James, and John – the three He chose out of the twelve disciples to accompany

Him on a prayer vigil on a mountain and in a garden. On both occasions the three became sleepy and dozed off. Yet, each time, Jesus was having a vital, extraordinary encounter with heaven. On the first occasion the glory of God came down and He talked with Moses and Elijah, as well as His Father. In the second, He was battling with the powers of darkness and with the horror of what He was about to go through. Through both, He wanted to share His experience with His three friends and, in the process, teach them something more about the deep things of God, available to us through prayer. In one experience, God was very much present; in the other, He seemed to be absent. One was glorious, and His face shone; the other was agonizing, and His faith was tested. These extremes of prayer, when heaven and earth are joined as one, are the substance of our ongoing communion with God. Prayer is never ordinary; it is always extraordinary!

Prayer triplets – a tool for today's Church in all cultures – are a God-given concept to help His Church grow and to improve the prayer experience of ordinary Christians. I feel immensely privileged to have been God's modern-day channel to bring this into existence, at least in my own country, Britain.

Notes

1. Brian Mills, *Three Times Three Equals Twelve: God's Strategy for Church Growth through Prayer Triplets* (Kingsway, 1986).

CHAPTER 4

LIGHT IN EVERY STREET

> You are the light of the world. A city on a hill cannot be hidden … Let your light shine before men, that they may see your good deeds and praise your Father in heaven.
>
> (Matthew 5:14, 16)

WE ARE CALLED TO BE LIGHTS to the world. Not dim and distant lights; not fading and flickering lights; not lights on one moment and off the next. But lights that light up the world around, like a city on a hill. Many have been the times when I have traveled by road across Salisbury Plain in the south of England late at night. The plain is a sparsely populated area, actually fairly high up. At night it used to be lit up – by the orange glow from a town called Andover, which is located in a valley! I used to see this light from over forty miles away, and think about this verse and the purpose of God behind it.

Jesus wants His disciples to be like Him. He said of Himself,

> I am the light of the world. Whoever follows me will never walk in darkness, but will have the light of life.
>
> (John 8:12)

But He says to His disciples, "You are the light of the world." We and He are to shine as lights in the darkness. The only way that can happen is for us to have the life of Christ so evident in us that, consciously or unconsciously, we cannot help but shine. He never said of Himself, "I'll be a shining light today, but not tomorrow." He couldn't help but be the Light of God in a world of darkness. Not to be light was inconsistent with His nature.

This comparison between light and darkness is a recurring theme throughout Scripture, in both Old and New Testaments. The world is viewed as full of darkness. But we, as God's followers, are viewed as full of light. Not to let our light shine should also be inconsistent with our spiritual nature and our profession to be His followers. Light is light; it is not darkness. How strange that we Westerners seem to do all we can to shade or hide our light, or even to protest sometimes that it is not there! In contrast, in many other parts of the world, Christians stand out as spontaneous witnesses. They can't help but let their light shine. Christ bubbles out of them. The Holy Spirit is radiating Jesus through their lives. Jesus says we are to "let" our light shine. It is already there, so by implication, we should not hide it.

We can't "make" our light shine. Either Christ is in us or He isn't. If He is in us, then the Holy Spirit within us reflects the Lord's glory through our eyes, mouth, hands, feet – in fact every part of our "being." We can't pretend to be Christians and expect that a light will shine.

We once had an occult plant in our church (that is, someone who is sent into the church to bring a wrong influence), but we didn't know she was one at first. However, several of us were suspicious. She passed herself off as a Christian and even came to prayer meetings. But her words and actions didn't ring true. There was something missing – and that had to be that Christ was not in her life. Many people who attend churches believe that by so doing they are Christians.

But that is not necessarily true. Billy Graham used to say, "If you are born in a garage, that doesn't make you a car." By the same criterion, if one attends a church, one is not *per se* a Christian. Similarly, if I attend a football match, it doesn't make me a footballer!

Although we can't make His light shine within us without having Christ in us, if we do have Christ's life within us we can prevent that light from shining. This is called "grieving" or "quenching" the Holy Spirit. By being hesitant, afraid of what others might think or say, or by choosing not to be open about our faith because we prefer to try and be worldly when "in the world", and "Christianly" when with Christians, we can prevent His light from shining.

A few years after the "era" of prayer triplets in Britain, I began to think of Christian homes (and not just Christian people) being lights to their community. At the time, 10 percent of the British population on average attended churches on Sundays. But what were they doing the rest of the week? Our light seemed to shine through our coming together with one another in worship and service on Sundays, or at certain other seasons (like Christmas and Easter) or events (like a joint church mission). Apart from that, the rest of the world was almost unconscious of the message of the gospel or the reality of people's faith. Sunday aggregate church attendances were ten times greater than Saturday aggregate attendances at professional football matches, yet the media didn't notice what churches did unless they joined together for something large and significant. Even then, there was no guarantee that the event would be newsworthy. So to talk of our light shining to the world could only be seen as an occasional thing. There must be some other way or time or place when we could be lights.

The average Christian in postmodern Britain often feels intimidated by the secular pressure around. Few know how to engage with the world and to be open with their faith, when the climate increasingly is one of ridicule, intolerance, discrimination, and sometimes of opposition. There has to be another way.

I have been in many top-level discussions over the years, about the need to make our faith relevant. We've thought and talked a lot about strategy, about church planting, about the stimulus of events to help ordinary Christians feel comfortable about gossiping the gospel. But all the time, we seem to confine the discussion to special events or programs. Where was the possibility, and the evidence, of us, as ordinary Christians, being the lights that God and Christ intended us to be?

Don't get me wrong. I'm not saying that these events and programs were unimportant. In the absence of ongoing faith-sharing they have been extremely important for the Church in Britain. The Billy Graham and Luis Palau missions of the 1980s brought tens of thousands of people to faith in Christ and continued to reap a harvest long afterwards. Projects such as those mounted in the 1990s by the combined Pentecostal denominations have also been productive in inspiring Christians to be witnesses, and in the fruit that followed. We've had large-scale literature distributions, but the hype associated with these has almost always failed to live up to the predictions made. The Challenge 2000 church-planting vision produced its spate of new churches and kick-started a process of discussions, training, and vision that continues in many denominations. March for Jesus has brought us out onto the streets in colorful displays of unity, praise, prayer, and witness. They've all been good while they lasted, and played their part in stirring us Christians up. I've personally been involved in all of these, and more besides, at national level for the past twenty or thirty years. But we still have not managed to *continue* being the lights that these events help us to be.

So what is missing? Opportunities on a regular basis for us to be together as Christians in small groups and to interact in some continuous way with those around us.

One day, David Pawson (an internationally renowned Bible teacher and a personal friend) and I went for a walk together near his home – something we used to do fairly regularly. We used to talk about the things concerning us. "What I believe we need," I began to say, "and what God has been speaking to me about, is a light in every street." "Did you know I have been preaching about that recently?" he responded. And so started an intriguing conversation.

A few weeks later, Nick Cuthbert (a Birmingham-based church leader) and I were traveling together by car. We started to share, and I said the same thing.

"Did you know I've written about that in my new book?" he responded. And so started another intriguing conversation! I've discovered that when God gives a seed-thought about what needs to happen, He doesn't give it to just one of His servants. He plants the seed in the hearts of many of His servants and waits to see who will act on it! He speaks to us and waits for us not only to hear Him, but to do what He's asking.

This was the inspiration I needed. And so, through the Evangelical Alliance, we launched Light in Every Street. It was simple really. We were merely sowing seeds of a vision and waiting to see who would respond, and how it would develop. We deliberately steered away from making it a program. We produced a four-page colorful leaflet, setting out the vision in a challenging way. We adapted the prayer triplet cards to incorporate a "light in every street" element.

The intention was to encourage Christians living in the same street to begin to meet together to pray for their non-Christian neighbors and friends. Out of that prayer, we had found, God would open up doors of opportunity for faith-sharing or neighborly action. We took encouragement from the biggest church in the world, Yoido Full Gospel Church in Seoul, Korea, which had grown to a membership of about 700,000 by encouraging its members to meet together in small groups to pray. They would then be encouraged to look for the crisis points in the community and to follow up with action. If a doctor calls at a local address, or a police car, or an ambulance, or a funeral director, or a wedding car, or a removal van – each reflects a crisis of some sort within the household. So Christians were encouraged not only to pray, but also to call and offer assistance to that family. Then, if they had no further contact, they would call back within two weeks to see how things were. If things had changed, and this had been the result of prayer, then a natural opportunity for faith-sharing presented itself. I discovered that this was the principal reason for the growth of what we now recognize as one of the main twentieth-century expressions of cell church.

Once the Light in Every Street vision was launched, through magazine articles, speaking engagements, and the release of materials, we began to hear how God was quickening the vision into action. Some groups were started between Christians of different denominations. Sometimes a church would adopt the idea and encourage all its members to pray for their neighbors. Sometimes a single family would pray intentionally for people with whom they had everyday contact, like the milkman, the postman, the paper boy, and the neighbors on either side.

A church in Wigan began to pray for the streets in their parish. They then would visit specific streets with an introductory leaflet, announcing that they would call two weeks later, when there would be a prayer group assigned to that street. They were amazed at the readiness of people to ask for prayer on the second visit. On the basis of this church's initiative, Christian Publicity Organisation reproduced the materials used to encourage other churches and places to do the same.

Another church, in Conisborough, Yorkshire, invited me to come and lead a Light in Every Street weekend. During the first teaching service, the lights were turned out; I lit a candle, then lit two more. Those holding them then lit two more each, and so on until sixty-five candles were lit and the darkened church was filled with light. Why sixty-five? That was the number of people who had signed up to pray for their neighbors. One of these had seen ten of her neighbors converted. The whole initiative spawned a number of social action projects in the town. And those whose prayers did not seem to be answered then linked together with the successful pray-ers to pray for breakthrough. Inevitably that church saw a spate of conversions and began to grow rapidly. It had to train people to pray with others. A book was compiled of the testimonies of people who had come to faith in the town through this Light in Every Street approach.

There was no uniform way in which the vision was picked up, but there was inbuilt flexibility for a variety of approaches. Other initiatives of a similar kind began to appear. There was Good News Down Your Street, a home-based evangelism training program for local churches to adopt, based on making neighborhood witness become a reality. This became a well-used slogan which was adopted by many of the more traditional churches. The program also included materials produced to enable everyone to do things in the way that the originators had.

The Together for Birmingham team (now defunct) launched a vision for 10,000 neighborhood prayer watches – people who would commit to praying for their neighbors and keeping spiritual watch over their street. This came out of a vision that initially was birthed through the Leeds expression of Challenge 2000. Stickers proclaiming "Neighborhood Prayer Watch" were produced for people to stick on their doors or windows. Visions like this need to be sustained and continually encouraged if they are to succeed.

The vision needs to be birthed in hundreds of churches if it is going to be effective and not confined to a few churches.

One year, March for Jesus introduced a prayer-walking element focused on people's neighborhood. Folk were asked to commit to praying for their street on the March for Jesus Day. As it happens, thousands of Christians throughout the country responded and on that day walked and prayed through their own neighborhoods. But one day of prayer is insufficient. If we want to be lights for God in our neighborhood, we need to keep on praying.

Ed Silvoso, the Argentinian preacher whom God has used so much in this country, and whose book *That None Should Perish*[1] has been key in helping people look at their city, also made a contribution. He started to speak about raising up "lighthouses of prayer" in our neighborhoods. He urged Christians to start praying for five homes to their right and five homes to their left, and for eleven homes opposite them. It only required 5 percent of homes doing this to cover the country with prayer. Statistically that is realistic. If 10 percent of the population are church attenders, then it should be manageable to get 5 percent of homes praying for their neighbors. If every Christian family became a lighthouse like that, we potentially could have lights in every street!

The common factor in all these ideas was the intention to help us become envisioned towards the same purpose. These visions and programs did not emerge at the same time, but each emerged about two to three years after the previous vision. In other words, God was speaking loudly and clearly to His Church in Britain about the same thing over a period of years. From this we can take it that He really does want us to be lights in our street!

Then there was Alpha! Although not focused on streets *per se*, the purpose and the results have been very similar. Alpha suppers have helped to attract interested non-

Christians to encounter our faith. It has majored on small groups to do this. Most groups have been church-based, but they could just as well be neighborhood-based. Consequently tens of thousands of people have come to faith in God and become involved in churches of all denominations. The only difference is that Alpha seems to have outlasted all the other visions and has been going for more than ten years. Why? Can it be that the organizers have tenaciously stuck to their vision and built around it a program? They haven't waited for Christians to adopt or adapt a vision. They have spelled out how it will work. It has worked, even though the spontaneity of being a light for Jesus is not essential to its success.

We Christians need incentives, it would appear. We don't do things by commitment, but by incentive. We need to see that we are not on our own in doing something, but are part of the bigger picture. That bigger picture is that other Christians are doing the same thing at the same time in the same area. It doesn't need to be nationwide, but it does need to be area-wide. And that's why Light in Every Street is still an attractive possibility.

Notes

1. Ed Silvoso, *That None Should Perish: How to Reach Entire Cities for Christ Through Prayer Evangelism* (Regal Books, a division of Gospel Light, 1994).

CHAPTER 5

PRAYING BEHIND THE SCENES

_I_F WE SEE PRAYER merely as an exercise in personal devotion, we shall miss so much of what God intends for us. Of course, prayer is the principal means of our fellowship and relationship with God. Without it we shall be starved spiritually. And without that personal life of prayer, any other form will be less than adequate and unsatisfying.

Prayer is, above all, our means of enjoying and fostering our relationship with God. But it is also the means God has given us for getting His will done on earth. When I consider prayer, I think of the cross. It has a vertical spar. Prayer is an upward relational activity whereby I can draw closer to my Father in heaven. I need to worship Him (John 4:23–24), to love Him (1 John 4:7–21), to appreciate all His attributes, and to get to know Him better (Ephesians 1:17). I need to hear His voice (Revelation 3:20), to learn what is on His heart, and to see things from His heavenly perspective (Ephesians 2:6–7). Prayer to God is for me a vital, daily, personal experience. I often read His Word and use that as a vehicle for prayer. What better than the Psalms for this? Today I read most of Psalm 119 out loud, using the phrases to reflect my desire for knowing Him better.

The cross also has a horizontal spar. That reminds me that God is also concerned for His Church to grow and for His Kingdom to be extended. So prayer also has an outward focus. Scripture envisages the time when the knowledge of the glory of the Lord will cover the earth, as the waters cover the sea (Habakkuk 2:14). Are we praying for that? It also envisages a time when the gospel of the Kingdom will be preached in the whole world (Matthew 24:14) to every tribe, people, and language group. Are we praying for that? Jesus commissioned His disciples to go into all the world, even to the uttermost parts of the earth (Matthew 28:19; Mark 16:15–16; Acts 1:8) and preach the gospel. Are we praying towards and for that?

Sometimes corporate prayer is seen as boring because the participants haven't caught in their spirits the big picture. When we merely pray "God bless" prayers, we fail to enter into the concerns of heaven. But when we pray from God's perspective, with Scripture and His promises being articulated, then prayer takes on a whole new meaning. Some of the most exciting corporate gatherings for prayer that I have been involved in relate to the big picture – getting the will of God done in places and among people where the needs are blatantly obvious.

As a young Christian leader, in my first ministry job with a missionary society focused on Central Asia, I was also asked to take on the leadership of the youth work at the church I attended in Balham, South London. Simultaneously with this, a couple of gangs started coming to our youth group. Nobody knew why they came; they just turned up. One of these was the notorious Lavender Hill Mob, about whom a film had been made. These teenagers brought with them all their values, hang-ups, practices, hatreds, and rebellion towards authority. It was a severe challenge, and it was my responsibility to respond. On the one hand, we had Christian parents rightly concerned for the safety of their own children and what they might get drawn into. On the other hand, we had to look after the church property in which we were meeting. And most important of all, we had to get know these youngsters whom God had sent into our midst, and witness to them of the love of God.

On youth nights, I needed to have my eyes everywhere. It was not uncommon to find two young teenagers copulating on church premises. We had to break up fights, when the knuckle dusters would come out. We had to guard against individuals hiding on the premises. We had some good sports equipment and attractive young Christian girls. We saw anger explode into the punching of holes in the ceiling of our counseling and prayer room.

To their credit, the older people in the church said, "We will come to the church and pray every Friday whilst the youth club is on." And they did. Even some of those I thought were out-of-touch elderly spinsters came regularly and gave themselves to pray. It was to their credit that, once this began to happen, Friday nights became much easier to run, problems almost disappeared, and we got to know these youngsters much better and more quickly. Just as suddenly as they began to come, the gangs would leave. And other gangs would come in their place. It seemed that our youth group was the talk of the gangs. I asked one of the leaders, who had a criminal record, why they came. "Something to do in a place where we're accepted," he said. Our young people were brilliant! They drew alongside these needy contemporaries, played games with them, witnessed to them, and yes, in a way, loved them.

It was there that I first learned the importance of prayer at the same time, and preferably at the same place, as the action. Many times since then, I have seen prayer like this being so significant. I've also seen where evangelism and church-planting efforts, done with the best will in the world and with the latest techniques, but without this kind of praying, achieve far less than the investment of time, effort, and ingenuity warranted.

Many years later I was visiting a revival area in Brazil. Here I could see so clearly the connection between this kind of praying and the obvious blessing of God. In Los Povos (Light to the People) Church in Goiania, intercessors would be praying virtually around the clock. They had an intercessory team with a variety of assignments. Before the major church services, they would come together for a couple of hours to pray. Whilst the services were on, they would be standing around the outer gangways of the church at an arm's length from each other, praying. There would be a small prayer team on the platform, just to cover the speakers. Consequently the services there were full of the presence and power of God. We saw extraordinary things happen. Whenever people came forward in response to a public appeal these intercessors, each wearing an intercessor's T-shirt, would spring into action to pray with individuals. If demons started to manifest, which they often did, the spiritual warfare team would immediately gather round. Here prayer and action went together. No wonder that church was large and growing.

Why is the Church not growing in Britain? We all have our reasons – and sometimes our excuses. But maybe one of the chief reasons is that we don't take prayer seriously, nor do we understand the spiritual world adequately. Do we not believe in prayer? Do we think God only works somewhere else in the world? I sometimes wonder if the activities we engage in within our churches are merely seen as that – activities of the Church. We fail to see them as potential places and occasions for people to meet with God. What if, in every church, there was a prayer group in action covering every single activity – at the time the activity was occurring? I reckon we would see a lot more fruit, and experience much less hassle. If we believe an activity is important to have, then it is important to be prayed over. And if we look to see God at work, then Satan himself will make sure he is also at work. Prayer is the only way we can counter his influence!

My learning curve continued under the inspiring example of the late Dr Alan Redpath. As chairman of the prayer committee during the Mission England meetings in 1984 at Villa Park, Birmingham, Alan would, night after night, lead the prayer team throughout the time that the meetings were in progress. We had similar prayer teams at the other venues too, but here in Birmingham it was like a power house – a boiler room!

Later, in 1989, when Billy Graham spoke at mission meetings in London, I was prayer chairman. So, at Upton Park, Crystal Palace, and Earls Court we had on-site prayer teams in action for five hours every evening. At Crystal Palace the prayer room became the most exciting place to be. We had a beautiful location – the press box! We could see everything and pray for what we saw, as well as what God told us to pray for. Members of the committee would come off the platform to join us. "It's more eventful here than there," they said.

The mission meetings coincided with the worst traffic chaos imaginable. All forms of public transport – trains, underground and buses – were subject to strikes. So the only ways of getting to and from the meetings were by car and coach. The roads around Crystal Palace were log-jammed. For the first time in the experience of the Billy Graham team, we had to postpone the start of the meetings. Police helicopters hovered overhead and relayed to one of our staff, stationed outside the prayer room, the information about where the worst jam was, and we then prayed to remove the traffic blockages. Miraculously the traffic chaos cleared, so that the meetings started only half an hour late!

Later, at Earls Court, we had about fifty people on duty in the prayer room each night. The evangelistic meetings were due to be transmitted by satellite to over 600 places throughout the United Kingdom and to thirty nations of Africa. Ten of those nations were due to transmit the meetings live over their television networks. The rest would record them for subsequent transmission.

On the first evening of transmission, the secretary for the late Bob Williams, who was the Graham team's coordinator, dashed into the prayer room. "We've lost all the power to Africa, and there's only eight minutes to go!" she blurted out.

I looked at my watch. "It's only five minutes now, but still plenty of time for God to work," I replied. I interrupted the prayer meeting and told them the problem. "We've got to save Africa!" I said. The meeting erupted into one of the best times of simultaneous audible prayer I had ever been part of!

The secretary, from India, remarked, "I didn't know you prayed like this in England."

"Neither did I," I replied. "But isn't it wonderful?"

Ten minutes later I slipped out of the prayer room to go to the transmission control center to find out what had happened. The power was back on. "But these highly skilled technicians – the best in Europe – couldn't find what went wrong, and are scared lest the power goes again," commented Bob Williams.

"I know who got the power restored," I said, "but we'll keep praying anyway."

A cheer went up in the prayer room as I reported what had happened. Then we split into three groups for the rest of the evening – one praying for the satellite transmissions to Africa, another praying for the hundreds of video centers throughout the UK, and the third praying for everything in Earls Court. A few weeks later I was at a conference in

Korea and was thrilled to hear reports there of the thousands who had given their lives to Christ through watching the satellite transmissions to Liberia from London. "Thank you, Lord," I breathed.

Since that time, at every major event for which I had responsibility as prayer leader, the mounting of a prayer team has been a key contribution to the blessing experienced. The DAWN conferences in Birmingham and Nottingham in the 1990s both had on-site intercessors who came to the event just to pray. They were supplemented by intercessors from the successful prayer movements in both those cities. For all involved, it was an exhilarating experience. Part of the responsibility of the prayer team was to pray for participants; any who came into the prayer room were offered prayer. It was wonderful to see these leaders receiving words of knowledge about their ministry, church, or life from praying Christians who had no knowledge of them or their background.

Another part of our responsibility was to cover all aspects of the conference. We would be in prayer during all plenary sessions, and had a couple of our number detailed as runners. They would go "to and fro" between the prayer room and the main auditorium. Frequently we would be praying about issues a mere five minutes before they were spoken about on the platform. At other times we would experience exactly what was being experienced in the plenary session. If things were "flat," we would be sensing it. If there was a battle going on, we would sense it too. If speakers were experiencing a hard time in ministering, we would pray them through to fluency and anointing. We would also assign ourselves to the venues for various regional meetings or workshops.

Why are these things important? Well, if we are really serious about seeing the Kingdom of God come in every area of life, then spiritual factors will come into play to

hinder God's purposes from being fulfilled. During preparations for the Graham meetings in 1989 we discovered that
Satanists had moved to buy homes around the outskirts
of London so that they could form a satanic ring around
London. From these homes it was their intention to pray
confusion into our ranks and issue curses against God and
His Christ into the spiritual atmosphere. They viewed us as
their enemies, so they developed a strategy to oppose us.

We are naive if we think that the servants of Satan,
and practitioners of the occult in various forms, are either
unaware or disinterested in what the Church does. If they
wish to advance their kingdom (and they do), they will be
dead set against us advancing God's Kingdom. That's one
reason for us to pray!

But also, if we are really serious about seeing fruit that
will last, we need to prepare people's hearts, their homes,
their surroundings by prayer, so that the Word sown into
their hearts will not fall on stony ground.

In other parts of the world, Christians understand
these principles very well. I have witnessed the effectiveness of full-time around-the-clock prayer teams at
the Lausanne Congress in Manila, Philippines in 1989;
at the Gideon's Army meeting of the Spiritual Warfare
Network in Seoul, Korea in 1993; at the meetings of the
Global Consultation on World Evangelization (GCOWE)
in 1995, also in Seoul, Korea; and at assemblies of Evan-
gelicals organized by the Evangelical Alliance in the UK
and by the European Alliance in Hungary. There was a
prayer team for the Explo 2000 meetings in Switzerland,
held over the days leading up to and beyond the turn of
the new millennium. Plenary meetings were being shown
by satellite to a worldwide audience of 30 million people. We also mounted a twenty-four-hour prayer team at
the International Prayer Leaders' Consultation in Cape
Town, South Africa in 2002.

Korea was interesting. Well over 500 churches have "prayer mountains" in Korea, where prayer occurs twenty-four hours a day. During my first visit there, we stayed at the "Hilton" of prayer mountains, owned by the Kwang Lim Methodist Church – the largest in the world. The Koreans had provided us Westerners with beds. They happened to be hard, narrow army beds! We slept about twenty to a room. That first night I couldn't sleep, even though I was tired from traveling. At 1 a.m. the Spirit of God said to me, "You are on a prayer mountain – what do you do on a prayer mountain?" So I got up and crept down the corridor to seek out a prayer cubicle, of which there were about a hundred, each of them about 1 meter square with a cushion on the floor. An American lady was slipping out of the women's dormitory at the same time for the same reason. So we prayed with each other for a few minutes, and then went to our assignments. For three hours I had a glorious time of fellowship with God on my own – without falling asleep.

Then at 4 a.m., the Spirit of God said, "You can go to bed now." Obediently I crept out, only to discover that the corridors were full of people passing one another! God had set up His own night shift of prayer. And we all had had similar experiences. Those of us going back to our beds were being replaced by those whom God had awakened to be on spiritual guard, and to have fellowship with Himself. So that prayer conference really did begin in prayer! We had a prayer team from the nations supporting us as we met in various sessions, and they also set up a night shift throughout the conference.

In 1995, fifty child intercessors were included in the prayer team. One day the prayer track met together, and for one session we met in regional groups. These children were assigned in pairs to go and pray in each venue. I was leading the European group. In walked two twelve-year-old boys, who started praying in a most mature way for us as a group and for different individuals. All of us were overwhelmed with the insight and power of their praying.

I have to say that sometimes I have detected only a mild tolerance of the need for a prayer team by the leadership of conferences or events. This has sometimes manifested itself as dishonoring the intercessors, particularly so in events where Westerners have been in charge. That leads me to the conclusion that many Westerners do not understand the connection between prayer and God's blessing. Nor do we fully understand that we operate in a spiritual world, of which the natural, material world is a part, not the other way around. In this spiritual world, the weapons of our warfare are spiritual. Those Christians working in places of revival wouldn't dream of not having a prayer team.

So I draw the conclusion that, if we want to receive the blessing of God in our nation on a massive scale, we must take prayer more seriously. George Carey, the former Archbishop of Canterbury, once said, "Show me a church that takes prayer seriously and I'll show you a church that is successful." Prayer behind the scenes does not need to be treated as an incidental activity – a kind of side-show to placate the "spiritual elitists" (as they are sometimes referred to). Prayer must be seen as the essential prerequisite for experiencing the blessing of God in a large measure on efforts to advance His Kingdom.

CHAPTER 6

PRAYER WALKING
AND SPIRITUAL MAPPING

W E WERE PLANNING for our first March for Jesus in the town of Reading in southern England, where we used to live. At that time I was committed to helping to coordinate prayer and evangelism in the various congregations of Kings Church, as a member of the ministry team. One day God said to me, "You need to walk and pray along the route to be used."

March for Jesus was still in its infancy. I had joined the first ever march in the city of London in 1987. Graham Kendrick and I had traveled together on a tour called Pray for the Nation (sponsored by the Evangelical Alliance) to many of the seventy towns and cities I had visited throughout the UK in the year before – 1986. On one of these week-long journeys I listened to the first sample of some of the songs to be used as Graham shared his vision with me. We talked about prayer walking, marches etc., which to our knowledge were first beginning to be experienced by the Church at that time. I had heard of some of the women from the Lydia Fellowship going on a prayer walk around the commercial district of the City of London. But I had never been involved in a prayer walk myself.

So when God said, "I want you to organize a prayer walk around Reading," I had to ask Him how to go about it. As I prayed about this, He led me to invite folk from the churches to come together in a central venue; we chose Greyfriars Church, Reading, a key city-center venue. Then He said, "Plan for three routes, and when the people come together, split them into triplet groups for walking and praying." One evening, my wife Ruth and I walked together around the Reading streets along the three routes, asking God what He wanted to be prayed about. Each of the routes took in part of the planned route for the March for Jesus. We took note of both the positive and negative things – churches and pubs! We picked out some historic elements. We made a list of possible prayer topics and locations for each route, typed these up, and photocopied them.

God also told me that I needed to know something about the history of Reading and the influences that had helped to make it what it is today. I am not a historian, nor a researcher. I had never been into Reading's Central Library before. And I wasn't really sure what I was looking for. However, God led me to look at two significant books, both of which outlined the history of Reading. Reading had been a prosperous town throughout its history. In recent times it had become the capital of the high-tech industry in the Thames Valley of England. It had also been a religiously significant place. An abbey had been established there by Benedictine monks. Eventually they became corrupted by the wealth in the area and acquired as much of it as they could at the expense of the poor, so creating a local under-class. The monks became very rich. Later into the town came the Franciscans (the grey friars), who championed the cause of the poor. This, in turn, brought them into conflict with the Benedictine monks. Since that time the Church – both Protestant and Catholic – had experienced constant division in the town. Up until that year, all attempts at doing anything in a united way had been short-lived and superficial.

The Friday evening for the prayer walk soon arrived. Forty-five Christians came from over a dozen churches, exceeding my expectations! After an initial time of briefing and prayer, we went out in three teams of fifteen people each, which meant there were five triplet groups in each team. Each team leader had to appoint a scribe to record impressions, significant scriptures, prophetic pictures etc. We allowed ourselves an hour to walk the fairly short distance of each route. In reality we took more than two hours. Afterwards, we had to "knock the vicar up" and get him out of bed, since we had left our things in the church, which he had already locked!

When we debriefed, everyone was excited at what they had seen. Most had only ever seen their town as a place to do shopping. They had never before looked at the town with spiritual eyes. They saw the plight of the homeless, and the drunkenness and drug use among the young. Some wept as they related how God had impacted them and opened their eyes to the true state of things. They had never before realized what happened in the town center on a Friday night. New ministries into the town center were born out of that prayer walk – each on a joint church basis!

Two things stood out from all the feedback – that Reading was really prosperous (although that was pretty obvious), and that the Church was divided: Christians were divided from each other, and also from the needy on the streets. Then I shared what I had discovered about the history of Reading.

There have been many other prayer walks in and around Reading since that time, all of them involving Christians from different churches. We've walked the twenty-five

miles perimeter of the town boundary, claiming the town
for God. We've walked along the arterial routes from the
outskirts to the town center. We've been on various assignments at the invitation of different churches, seeking to
bring release to their communities. Lots of individuals and
churches have made prayer walking part of what they have
done regularly for a while. But that first walk was when we
"learned to walk spiritually."

Reading has changed. Gifts and ministries to the poor
of the town have captured the interest of the churches.
Christians are vitally involved in social work, the probation
service, education, and in the medical world. Churches
have reached out to asylum seekers. There is a pregnancy
counseling service called Lifeline, run by Christians from
several churches. Another ministry helps the poor and
the homeless. The Reading Boiler Room – initially an initiative for twenty-four-hour prayer – found itself in a unique
situation to reach out to hundreds of needy young people. Churches have mounted a witness at the now-famous
Reading Pop Festival. And a few years ago all churches
combined in a unique mission to the unchurched, called
Thames Valley Alive.

The distinctions have been broken down between the
Church and the world. They have also been broken down
between the churches. The leaders of various churches
across the denominational spectrum have been meeting
and praying together every Wednesday morning for several
years. Out of that prayer has developed a level of ongoing
cooperation in relation to the town that is unprecedented in
its history. God has answered prayer, and the barriers have
been broken down. Reading also has one of the highest
percentages of church attendance of anywhere in the UK.
Looking back, prayer has been the key.

Since then, I've walked and prayed in all kinds of situations around the world, including some of the world's

trouble spots. There is nowhere that we as Christians cannot go. Books have been written on prayer walking and prayer expeditions that have helped Christians around the world learn more and do more. Prayer journeys for on-site prayer teams have brought significant breakthroughs in some of the most difficult nations of the world. When God tells us to do something "new," we may be sure that He has also told others the same thing! That to me is a safeguard in my discerning how to recognize the "voice" as God's.

That first experience of prayer walking has resulted, for me, in opportunities for teaching on the topic in a variety of churches, towns, cities, and nations. When leading a day's teaching on spiritual warfare, I usually include a prayer walk for participants. We have a morning's teaching, spend the afternoon prayer walking and reporting back, and then have an evening of prayer for the local community based on what our research has produced.

We were doing this around Enfield, North London, one day. As a friend and I walked through the local park close to a stream and approaching a church, God started to tell me that the "spirit of death" was all around. It was so strong that I kept asking my companion, "What has been here? Has it been a graveyard? Is it something to do with the church? Has there been a massacre?" When reporting back later, someone told me that the area in question had been the burial place for the thousands who died in the Great Plague of London – hundreds of years previously! Why was God showing us this? Because blood still cried out from the land, and maybe also the spirits of the dead still inhabited the area, instead of having been dispatched to their eternal resting place.

That experience of prayer walking in Reading was also my first inadequate foray into what is now known as "spiritual mapping." The term wasn't in use then, but many of us were doing the mapping bit before the phrase was coined.

Today, many major on this as their contribution to the spiritual task facing the Church. Two of my colleagues, David
and Claire Sladden, have made the gathering of research
for the advance of the Kingdom of God their prime occupation. It has become invaluable for all that God has led us
into over the last ten years!

On spiritual mapping, David Sladden has written:

> Basic to the challenge of drawing up spiritual maps is under-
> standing how spiritual forces operate. This can be a problem
> for us, because our Western culture and education system,
> with their roots in the philosophy of ancient Greece, destroy
> our natural ability to see the spiritual world. In the non-West-
> ern world, however, everyone is aware of the spiritual realm
> – unless they have become completely Westernized. The
> loss of our spiritual sight and hearing is a real problem for us
> Westerners. The good news is that it is perfectly possible to
> recover them.
>
> A lot of Christians tell me they have great difficulty hearing
> the Lord's voice (not usually heard as an audible voice) – or
> knowing the Lord's voice from all the other voices, like their
> own thinking or what they hear "at church". Jesus made it
> clear not only that he himself heard his Father's voice (e.g.
> John 7:16) but that those who followed him – his "sheep" –
> would "know his voice" and "hear", or "listen", to it (John
> 10:4, 16). He also revealed the principle underlying his minis-
> try: "the Son can do nothing by himself; he can only do what
> he sees his Father doing, because whatever the Father does
> the Son also does" (John 5:19).[1]

So, foundational to spiritual mapping is an understanding of
the spiritual world around us – good and bad. And for this
we need to be able to hear the voice of God. He sees what
is going on in the spiritual realm, and His knowledge of
history is unparalleled!

What is "spiritual mapping"? Missions researcher George Otis Jr says, "Spiritual mapping involves superimposing our understanding of forces and events in the spiritual domain onto places and circumstances in the material world." This information is then applied through intensive prayer and strategic evangelism.

Looking at the detail of what is included in spiritual mapping, I have found the following guidelines and questions to be useful.

Historical data

Many towns and cities have strong historical traditions relating to wars, pagan festivals, and places of worship, which all serve to give them their character or personality. We need to identify influences that either contribute towards, or create barriers to, the spread of the gospel.

Who founded your city or town? Why was it established and where? What significance is there in names, crests, mascots etc.? How has the area developed? What has been its significant contribution? What are its reputation and character? What changes have occurred and why? Has there been a downside as well as an upside to its character? How have minorities been treated? Have there been wars, bloodshed, disasters, and treaties involving the area?

Solid contemporary information is obtainable from a variety of sources. Tourist boards may provide information on ceremonies and historic or occult sites. A local or university library or the national records office may also be consulted. Dossiers can be built up of news items from the local press. Or simply by using a search engine on the internet, one can discover a lot about the relevant history of a place. We look for clues and insights into that which gives the place its character and reputation. Inevitably there will also be a spiritual component to some of this.

Spiritual data

Non-Christian influences

Non-Christian religious practices impact the character and atmosphere of a city. What has characterized the area through its history? What non-Christian religions operate in the area today? Are there any New Age, occult or satanic groups and centers? Where are they located? What secret societies have been in the area?

Christian influences

When did Christianity enter the city or town and where did it start? Where are the main Christian centers located today? Has "the Church" been perceived as making a positive or negative contribution to the area? Is there a history of division, or cooperation? In what past conflicts has the Church figured prominently? Is the Church growing; if so, where? Are there areas where it has never really flourished? Have wrong covenants been made, which have implicated the Church? Have righteous covenants been made (as when a town is founded to honor God), which have been subsequently broken? For example, in New England, USA, many towns were founded by early pioneers who made a covenant with one another and before God. The city of Glasgow in Scotland adopted this prayer as their slogan: "O God, let Glasgow flourish by the preaching of your Word and the praising of your Name." Today that has been shortened to a mere "Let Glasgow flourish."

Divine revelation

What has God shown individuals visiting the city? What has He shown churches, intercessors, or leaders about the prevailing influences, spirits, or powers over the city or town? Have these messages been shared or tested? Have the spiritual leaders made a connection between such revelations and ongoing united prayer? What have been the results? Have they been sustained? If God gives us revelation then it has to be used if it is to fulfill its intention. Often revelation from God provides us with clues which connect with the historical reality.

Physical data

Demographic
What is the composition of the population: location, numbers, ethnic distribution, age etc.? This can be broken down by district, ward, or enumeration district and may be obtainable from census information, available in government departments. This information will help in targeting evangelism and church planting towards particular ethnic or need-oriented people and groups, and into areas where there are few, if any, churches.

Geographic
Do geographic features have any bearing on the influences in the area? Have those features been invested with significance through religious importance being placed on them? Are there areas which have always been known for their poverty, wealth, prostitution, crime etc.? Some churches have discovered that major trunk roads and rivers become effective barriers to the influence of the church, where the church is on one side and the people on the other! Mountains and hills still become used as "high places," as they were in Canaanite practices in Old Testament times. Multistorey car parks sometimes fulfill an equivalent function for low-lying areas!

Architectural
Is there any significance attached to particular architecture like statues, gargoyles, museums, or church buildings

that might have bearing on the spiritual life of the area? Why are some cities laid out with Masonic symbols? What importance should be placed on obelisks? Some years ago, intercessors from the Lydia Fellowship were going to Liverpool for a prayer day. Two ladies, independently of each other, were directed to the story of Dagon, the Philistine god who was half man, half fish (see 1 Samuel 5:1–5). On arrival in Liverpool they discovered that the mosaic on the floor of the council chamber was of a creature resembling Dagon! Why was that put there, and when?

What should be done with the information?

Compile dossiers of these various components. Plot them on a map, where practical. By building up layer upon layer of such information, one may find common factors and threads in certain parts of the area which will provide more understanding about the factors that make certain places less open to the gospel than others.

I've found it helpful to ask the researchers among us not to disclose what they have found until those more involved in real intercession have sought God's face and prayed over the area. Sometimes the revelation gained through such prayer will highlight the need for further research or confirm the rightness of what has been discovered. But not all research is relevant to the spiritual task. However, research and revelation together should provide an ongoing agenda for prayer in relation to the spiritual factors that inhibit growth.

Leaders and intercessors should engage in a variety of prayer, intercession, and warfare throughout the city, using this data. They then need to encourage every Christian to be involved in praying, at the level they feel comfortable. There is no room for elitism in prayer; we are all needed. But we do have different experiences, and we may have different heavenly assignments. In a modern army the foot-soldiers and the intelligence corps have completely different functions, but they are both needed and depend on each other, recognizing each other's distinctives in the same army and operation. So too with the spiritual!

Those engaging in more strategic spiritual warfare will need to go through a process of strong and maybe prolonged prayer. This may involve personal and corporate repentance, leading to humility and holiness of life. They will need to recruit some back-up prayer before engaging in any confrontation over demonic issues or with demonic forces.

The methodology of spiritual warfare principally has to do with uplifting the name of Jesus, proclamation of the Word of God, confronting powers of darkness where known, and prophetic acts. There will be a negative element – opposing what is evil – and taking our stand against the devil's evil schemes. There will also be a positive element, that is, the affirmation in and through prayer of the opposite values to those of the spirit that is being encountered. Discovering, affirming, and praying for the city's redemptive gifts will sometimes be a common element. And calling forth the legacy of spiritual good from the past may also occur. God's plan of action and timing should be sought and followed. Whatever the methodology, the end should be the same: to pray God's blessing on the city and its people, its institutions, and its churches.

Notes

1. Taken from David Sladden, *Partnering in Prayer* (a work in progress).

CHAPTER 7

SPIRITUAL WARFARE
OVER OUR CITIES

———————— ≈ ————————

GOD LOVES CITIES, even though they are the creation of human beings. In them live many thousands, and sometimes millions, of people. And though all kinds of wrong activities occur in them and the sin of many is apparent, God still loves them. At least He responds to the prayers of His servants when they plead before Him on behalf of cities.

Consider Abraham's prayer for the twin cities of the plain, cities whose infamy has continued to the present day: Sodom and Gomorrah (see Genesis 18:20–33). Think of Babylon, also notorious in the annals of human history. Daniel prayed in it, even for those whose spiritual allegiance was diametrically different from his (see Daniel 2:18–23). Jeremiah wrote to the Jewish elders in exile in Babylon, giving God's prophetic word to them:

> Seek the peace and prosperity of the city to which I have carried you into exile. Pray to the LORD for it.
>
> (Jeremiah 29:7)

Jerusalem is probably the most prayed-for and prayed-in city on earth. Nehemiah, Daniel, Ezra, David, and Solomon all prayed for it and, apart from Daniel, in it. There the Savior of the world prayed what has been described as the greatest prayer ever prayed:

> Father, forgive them, for they do not know what they are doing.
>
> (Luke 23:34)

Jesus wept over Jerusalem and its disobedient and unresponsive people. There the fledgling Church, made up of fearful but obedient disciples, prayed. There the Holy Spirit was poured out on them.

But what about today? Where are the people who pray the will of God for their city? Where are those who will intercede as these prophets did? Where are those who will bring God's word to cities and not merely to the people in them? How are we to bring change to cities, and what place does the Church of God have to play in this process?

Some years ago I became concerned that we saw such little impact with the gospel in cities. If we were fortunate to have a big mission, with Billy Graham or another famous evangelist, we might for a season see a difference made, and thousands of people might have a conversion experience (most of these, however, were already churchgoers). But we saw little long-term impact and rarely any abiding change. Over the years, I have spent long hours walking the streets, knocking on people's doors, engaging in "visitation campaigns." Like many others, I have preached on street corners and in town squares. I have been with evangelists in town and city evangelism and on large housing estates. The thoroughness which has characterized such missions has often been commendable and the ingenuity shown both in the communication and the methodology has been admirable. But the fruit has been little. Although I have lived in cities most of my life, I confess that I have not liked being in them. I could find little to remind or point me to God, in contrast to the countryside. Maybe I failed to love my city as God loved it!

Anyway, I started to ask God questions about cities, and had discussions with some of my friends. How does God see cities? What does He want us to do about them? What are the spiritual forces at work in and over our cities? As mentioned in the previous chapters, God is showing me, more and more, that the real world is the spiritual world. The physical world is part of this. With our Western under-standing, however, we tend to view the physical world as the real world. And rarely do we acknowledge that there is a spiritual dimension to all of life.

From the word of God to the seven churches in the cities of Asia Minor in Revelation chapters 2 and 3, we learn quite a bit about how God saw those cities and by implication how we need to look at our cities today. God spoke to them through the angels *over* them, and His mes-sage was to the churches *in* them – those who represented Him within those cities.

Firstly, the letters are actually written to the "angel of the church in ..." Do our churches have angels assigned to them? I believe so – at least the Church as God sees it within a city. (The Church in the city is the sum total of all the Christian believers living there and the worshipping communities they are part of.) These angels are heavenly beings who are "ministering spirits sent to serve those who will inherit salvation" (Hebrews 1:14). That includes us – all of us who are joint "inheritors" with Christ. West-ern Christianity has almost edited out of its experience and vocabulary any reference to, or acknowledgment of, this amazing, huge, holy, radiant army of heavenly warriors who are sent from heaven to help us.

Spiritual warfare starts with God. There is a war going on in the heavenly realms, and there has been for centuries. The forces of heaven and of God are pitched against the forces of hell, who owe allegiance to Satan, a former archangel who lost his place in heaven because of pride (see Isaiah 14:12–17 and Revelation 12:7–9). Why would it be necessary for God to assign angels to churches in cities unless they were under threat from God's enemies?

This brings us to the second point. What was the substance of the message brought to each of those angels? Although there were some differences in the detail, the basic substance was the same. It had to deal with the sin of the church, and the already active work of Satan in the city. Although these were first-generation Christians, in the first century of the Church sin had entered. Sin, whether in our personal lives or in our corporate identity, weakens us, both in our ability to do the work of God and in our capacity to combat the work of Satan. If we tolerate sin, then Satan predominates. Sometimes that very sin, committed by God's own people, has provided an entry point for the control of Satan to be expressed to the detriment of both God's people (ourselves) and God. And that sin may become widespread – even endemic – among the surrounding population, because God's children have opened the door for that to happen. So the first message to the Church was "Repent!"

What sins are we talking about? The church in Ephesus had identified false apostles, whom they did not tolerate, and had lost their first love. That's all! Pergamum had sexual immorality and had tolerated the teaching of those who ate the wrong food – that which had been offered to idols. That's a bit more serious! In Sardis the church's reputation was no longer what it had been; they were only partially obedient. Laodicea had become lukewarm in their beliefs, materialistic and self-sufficient, and had tried to put a spin on their spirituality. In Thyatira a Jezebel figure was in their midst who was passing out her sexual favors and also the wrong food (a potent mixture for unsuspecting and gullible men!).

Come on, Church! We need to do some serious clearing-out of the skeletons in our corporate cupboards. How can we expect to do the work of God and fulfill the will of God if we continue to tolerate wrong attitudes, disunity, criticism, sexual immorality, pride, rebellion, and superficial obedience? How can we hope to combat the influence of Satan in society if we carry hidden baggage? How on earth will we experience revival and see transformation if there is no humbling of ourselves and confession of our sin, and turning from our wicked ways? If repentance doesn't happen among us, then, as the Church in the city (any city), we will have no grounds to do anything about the presence and influence of evil in the rest of the city.

Only Smyrna, who were victims of slander, and Philadelphia, who although weak had remained true to God's Word, had nothing negative said about them. Yet there were messages of warning to both of them to hold on, despite coming persecution and difficulties.

The messages to the seven churches also had to do with the work of Satan in the city as well as in the church. There was a synagogue of Satan in both Smyrna and Philadelphia – people who claimed to be Jews, but weren't. So that's why they were victims! Satan is still slandering God's people and seeking to weaken us from the inside if he can, just as he was in Smyrna and Philadelphia. The sect of the Nicolaitans – those who believed in eating food sacrificed to idols and in sexual immorality – was active in Ephesus and Pergamum. The person described as Jezebel in Thyatira (she was in the church!) was teaching "Satan's so-called deep secrets" (Revelation 2:24). And Pergamum was the center for emperor worship in the region. It was also the city where there was a physical altar, shaped like a huge seat, dedicated to the worship of Zeus. It was this which was referred to as the throne of Satan and the place where he lived (Revelation 2:13). What a reputation to have! It was a place of Roman idolatry, through which it appears that Satan had built a stronghold. So within one generation of being founded, these churches of Asia had been infiltrated by Satan.

Today the actual Pergamum altar is located in Berlin, Germany in the Pergamum Museum (as are the gates of the ancient city of Babylon). Discovered by German archaeologists in the late nineteenth century, it was shipped to Berlin and remained there through two world wars. Then Stalin had it relocated to Moscow shortly after the Second World War. Later Honecker, the East German president, asked for it to be returned to Germany. Some other altars built elsewhere in the world are styled on this one. It seems highly significant that so much time and attention has been given to this physical altar. The significance given to it and its replicas surely reflects its spiritual reputation from the first century AD. Where Satan has his physical location today is an open question.

How is it with us? With such pointed references to the work of Satan in these churches and in the cities, one would imagine that God intended us to take notice and look for what is happening with us. But we hardly raise an eyebrow at the infiltration of Satan into our churches and do not see the devil behind the persecution that so many face (see Revelation 2:10). The reality is that Satan is alive and well, and is active in our churches and in our cities. What are we doing to combat him and his influence? Of course he can only be present in one place at one time. But he has a network of fallen angels and evil spirits to do his bidding.

Satanism and witchcraft, New Age groups and practitioners, false religions and quasi-religious cults – these all flourish in our Western society. Whilst the Church has turned a blind eye to anything to do with the work of Satan and the spiritual war we are all in, Satan has spread his influence through myriads of groups and networks. Many of these "dark" groups target churches, bring curses against ministers and church property, pray for the breakdown of health and the break-up of marriages of Christian leaders, and do their utmost to oppose the work of the Church, to denigrate it to others, and to marginalize us in the media. Some of these New Age groups have also established themselves as "churches," so deluding the unsuspecting and unaware into a false spirituality. Some have infiltrated their way into existing churches and worked themselves into positions of leadership, from which they bring their false teaching. I have come across witchcraft "plants" in some churches (that is, individuals, usually women, sent in to sow discord and to seduce leaders).

We have to ask the question, Why? Why is Satan so active in our cities? There can be a variety of answers. Basically, he has been invited, either by groups who form and invite him to work in and through them, or by the opportunity Christians have knowingly or unknowingly given him in the past through unrepented sin, particularly that which is corporate.

My colleague Jeff Marks has had quite a bit to do with Salem, Massachusetts, in the USA. Named after Jeru-salem, it too was intended to be a city of peace. Its original founders entered into a covenant with God and with one another. Some years after its founding, the Christians broke covenant with God – not intentionally, of course, but in reality they did. Firstly, they were involved in the death of some Native Americans, particularly those who were described as "praying Indians," who had been converted under the ministry of missionary John Elliot. Secondly, they started accusing some of their womenfolk of involvement in witchcraft. As a result, the famous witch trials of the late seventeenth century ended in the death of those accused, some of whom

were undoubtedly Christians. So here were two examples
of Christians sinning against one another, even to the shedding of innocent blood.

Today Salem is regarded as the witchcraft capital of the
United States. Why? Those heavily into witchcraft persuaded
the city authorities that there was an economic "plus" for the
city if they should develop the town's historical heritage relating to witchcraft and the witch trials. Every Halloween tens
of thousands of people from around the world congregate
in Salem to experience witchcraft. Regular re-enactments of
the original trials take place – more than 300 years later!

Although there has been some progress in Salem as
Christians have prayed over the years, yet still the spiritual
battle rages. Some witches have been converted; others have
infiltrated churches; some Christian young people have been
enticed into the witchcraft web. Pastors and their families
have come under spiritual attack. A former church, taken
over and used by Satanists and renowned locally as "the
black house," has been recently re-purchased by a Christian
coalition and refurbished for the work of the Kingdom, as
a place of prayer and healing. The city of Salem, once in
the control of the witches, has slowly been wrested from
their grasp.

I was on a plane to Boston a couple of years ago, about
ten days before Halloween. I was going there for Christian purposes, including a prayer conference in Salem. As I
took my seat, the Holy Spirit said, "You are surrounded by
witches." Immediately I stood up and looked around, and
began to identify them. As I looked, I saw the tell-tale symbols around their necks, on their clothing, or in their eyes. It
seemed that they were all looking at me too. They seemed
to know that I knew who they were, and they knew who I
belonged to, I'm sure. It was an interesting flight!

There are many cities around the world where the
blend of historic and contemporary events, personal and

corporate sin, groups on earth and powers in heaven combine to create a spiritual cauldron and context where the gospel is hardly heard and where the light of God is dim. Are we to watch impotently? Or can we do something to change the spiritual atmosphere?

Through repentance and faith we can begin to take our stand against the devil and his schemes (Ephesians 6:11–12). As we seek and achieve the unity of God's people in prayer, we can then focus prayer on the various areas of the city and on the institutions in it. If we wish to see change, we need to ensure that people know their assignment from heaven and become committed to be on guard spiritually over their streets and tower blocks, their village, or their ethnic group. There is also a need for prayer groups to be committed to pray for the local government, schools and education, the business and banking community, the media and arts world, the judiciary and police force, and those involved in the medical world and caring professions. Preferably these prayer groups should be in the institutions as well as for them. Some also need to engage in prayer that relates to the perceived strongholds and activities of Satan and his earthly servants.

This is not a quick, easy fix. Prayer has to be sustained, and tactics will alter as the Holy Spirit directs. As we begin to see breakthrough, that is not the time to give up, but to press in. If we experience counter-attacks, then we know we are getting somewhere, so we redouble our efforts and increase the alertness of the spiritual army. We do not give up; we press on. At the same time, we can ask God to send his angels into battle against the principalities ruling over the area. We need to be strengthening our own resources by asking for prayer for one another. We have to maintain unity at all costs, so prayer for one another is essential.

The kind of prayer that is required may be beyond our previous experience. Let's not be hesitant about that. If we knew all there is to experience about prayer, we would have seen breakthroughs. God needs to take us beyond ourselves into a depth of repentance, forgiveness, intercession, travail, and waiting on Him. We will learn as we go. And God will be our teacher.

Satan is at work in our cities. We had better wake up to that fact and prepare God's children to do battle against the spread of evil influences and strategies. These affect masses of people, keeping them in spiritual blindness, holding them in all kinds of spiritual bondages. In some cases this is directly because of the stranglehold Satan has over institutions, geographical areas, and even the Church, not merely because of an individual's personal weaknesses.

In the previous chapter we looked at some of the ways of looking at our cities, through spiritual mapping. If we want to see lasting change, we have to engage with God and seek His strategy. Whilst there are principles and practices in praying that we can encourage, at the end of the day only God can give us the insight to know and do what is essential to see breakthrough. His method of achieving this may be different in each situation.

GODLY SUPERNATURAL POWERS – ANGELS

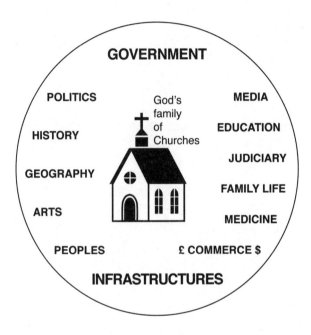

SUPERNATURAL EVIL POWERS

Profile of a City

CHAPTER 8

PRAYER AND THE HARVEST

———————— ≈ ————————

MANY OF US WANT TO SEE a spiritual harvest of astounding proportions. But harvests don't just happen! Months and years of planning and work precede every harvest.

Jesus, too, was looking for a harvest. When He saw the crowds looking harassed and helpless, leaderless and without a shepherd, He had compassion on them. But He saw beyond the immediacy of their needs. He saw a harvest, and told His disciples:

> Ask the Lord of the harvest therefore to send out workers into His harvest field.
>
> (Matthew 9:36–38)

Harvest time is always busy. If you have ever stayed on a farm at harvest time, you know that there is something for everyone to do; there is no room for spectators or passengers. The harvest has to be gathered in. And time is of the essence.

In Israel there are normally three harvests a year: the barley harvest in April/May, the wheat harvest in June/July, and the fruit harvest in September/October,

whereas in the similar latitude of the southern hemi-
sphere the equivalent harvests are reaped six months
later. In some countries there is more than one harvest of
each crop each year. Spain and Portugal have four orange
harvests a year (depending on the variety). Some plants
give multiple harvests in a year. In temperate climates
the harvest has to be gathered at just the right time, usually very quickly, and is dependent on the weather. In
other climates the middle of the day is not the ideal time
to harvest because of the overhead sun. Some harvests
are vulnerable to plagues of locusts or other insects, or
foxes and other animals. In some places there is a risk of
fire. So watchtowers, manned twenty-four hours a day,
are commonplace in certain areas. All this relates to the
type of harvest and its ingathering. When people think
of harvests, they are programmed to think of all the
problems. But when Jesus talked of harvest He looked at
the potential. As He was in Israel, He probably thought
of three harvests in a year.

When we think of what precedes the harvest, the list of
problems is much longer. One of my friends is a specialist
in soil testing. He can tell what kind of crop will grow in a
particular kind of soil. I told him what kind of soil I had in
my garden (clay), so he prescribed potatoes and gave me
five varieties to try in order to see which would crop the
best in my soil. Unfortunately the slugs ate all the roots!
Two years of experimentation and still no harvest! "Stick
to fruit above ground," he then advised me. (We already
had plum trees and blackcurrant bushes which provided a
prolific harvest!) The trouble is that spiritually we all want
instant results.

If they are planting cereal crops, farmers have to plow
the soil two or three times. Then they may have to harrow
it in order to rake out stones and weeds that would hinder
growth. Only then do they sow the crop. Then nature goes

to work, and the crop grows, but the farmer may have to spray the crops to prevent disease, or water them to aid growth. After the growth comes the ripening. Then finally it's time for the harvest!

Jesus links the natural harvest with the spiritual harvest in the parable of the sower (see Mark 4:1–20). He shows that He is fully aware of all the risks to the harvest. He identifies the active involvement of Satan, the rootless response of those who are superficial, the costs of persecution, and the cares and attractions of the world. But He is still expecting a harvest "thirty, sixty or even a hundred times what was sown"!

The implications for us are obvious. If farmers naturally have to put so much time and effort into preparing the harvest, then how much more should we, as we look for a spiritual harvest? The harvest of a crop is a partnership between human beings and God. People have to work, but God does the growing and the ripening, through nature – the combination of water, sun, and soil. So it is with the spiritual harvest. When we pray, it is like the plowing up of the fallow ground and the disposal of all things that lie in the way. Then we sow the seed (evangelism and witness). Then we pray some more, watching over the growing process and keeping unwanted visitors away. We water, by prayer, the seed sown in the right place. Then God brings forth the fruit.

Through the Billy Graham missions in England I had already seen how prayer had been so significant in relation to the conversion of individuals (see Chapter 3). Statistics show that around 80 percent of Christians owe their conversion to Christ to the prayers and friendship of others. Again and again we have seen the significance of prayer in relation to the harvest. But it was whilst I was involved with a church-planting movement called DAWN that God began to show me these simple lessons about harvesting.

DAWN (Discipling A Whole Nation) was worldwide in scope. A book written by Jim Montgomery entitled *Dawn 2000*[1] set out the vision for church-planting movements. Much of the thinking had come out of the Philippines where in 1974 Christians had set a target to see 50,000 churches planted in their country by the year 2000 – one for every *barangay* (village community). They reached their target of 50,000 churches some time in the late 1990s! By then, however, there were many more barangays. I was present when Philippine church leaders met together in the year 2000. They rejoiced at what had happened, but took notice of the parts of the country where they had failed to reach their target. They also set more targets for continued growth.

In the early 1990s a group of national leaders had come together to strategize for a huge church-planting program in England. I was invited onto the Challenge 2000 steering group for England to bring a prayer dimension into the strategy. Before I met with this group for the first time, I asked God what He wanted for England. I believe I heard God tell me, "Twenty thousand churches planted by the year 2000." When I arrived at my first steering group meeting I shared this, only to be met by amazed looks. The other group members had already been talking together and doing some strategy based on statistics. They had arrived at the same figure! So we all went to work, each with a lot to do to impart the vision to skeptical Christian leaders. Eventually the vision was accepted and the goals were adopted. Then we had to set about helping things to happen. People were trained, committees came into being, Christians started to work together, and momentum began to build.

Together with the help of Rachel Hickson, Faith Forster, David Sladden, and Bob Dunnett, we wrote a prayer manual called "Developing a Prayer Strategy," which was aimed at leaders. This spelled out the vision and suggested ways through prayer whereby the vision could become reality. It aimed to show that everyone's prayers were important and to illustrate how the targets could be achieved. It was up to the churches to implement the suggestions; all we could do was to impart the vision and sell the manuals. In a way, we were providing the seed and the instructions about how to prepare for the harvest! That prayer manual has since been updated for the twenty-first century. It has also been translated into a dozen languages for use around the world.[2] Regretfully, the whole vision and program in England ran out of steam and out of money from 1997 onwards. But to this day I still believe that we had heard from God; He wanted 20,000 churches started in England by the year 2000. That it apparently didn't happen wasn't His fault. We had our post-mortem. We had many reservations; we were all probably at fault in some ways. Some believe we were too ambitious and got our sums wrong! But I still believe the vision for the 1990s was right. If it was down solely to our human endeavor, then the project would have needed a much longer time frame and required more detailed planning. These were faith targets – and much faith was needed. Maybe our faith did not get exercised sufficiently. Maybe there was some skepticism, which is not a recipe for faith. In retrospect I also believe that many more churches were actually planted than appeared in the official statistics. New forms of church rarely appear in denominational figures.

After Jesus had the encounter with the woman at the well in Samaria (see John 4), He said to His disciples:

> Do you not say, "Four months more and then the harvest"? I tell you, open your eyes and look at the fields! They are ripe for harvest.
>
> (John 4:35)

Jesus had one encounter with a woman from a part of Israel that had been plagued by idolatry for centuries. It was a

spiritually barren and difficult region. The Jews traditionally saw difficulties with those from Samaria. Hence "Jews
do not associate with Samaritans" (John 4:9). Yet, through
that one encounter He saw a harvest, whereas His disciples
probably only saw problems. They saw Him talking with
a woman, a Samaritan woman at that, and one with loose
morals who had had five husbands and was with her sixth
man. It was natural for them to foresee problems. But Jesus
saw a spiritual harvest. No wonder that the resurrected
Christ, in commissioning these same disciples, reminded
them that, once the Holy Spirit came on them, Samaria was
to be part of their mandate (Acts 1:8).

Many of us, alas, look at the circumstances around us
and become discouraged by the obvious difficulties. We see
a lack of interest. We see increasing secularism. We work
with flawed people and limited resources. We face a crisis of
nerve; we have lost the will to witness. We have somehow
missed our way. Scripture says:

> Whoever watches the wind will not plant;
>> whoever looks at the clouds will not reap.
>
> (Ecclesiastes 11:4)

We need to see things from God's perspective. What does
He want and how does He want us to go about fulfilling
His purposes? With only five loaves and two fish to feed a
large crowd, the disciples saw a problem (see Mark 6:30–44).
"Send the people away so that they can ... buy themselves
something to eat" was their response. But Jesus saw an
opportunity: He had the people sit down and said to His
disciples, "You give them something to eat." We still have a
God who is "able to do immeasurably more than all we ask
or imagine, according to his power that is at work within
us" (Ephesians 3:20).

God responds to faith – faith in Him and in what He
can do. That is what pleases Him. In fact, "without faith

it is impossible to please God" (Hebrews 11:6). Nothing is accomplished without faith – faith in God and faith expressed in prayer. Where are the modern-day giants of faith who, like their predecessors, persevered against all the odds? Read again Hebrews 11 and ask God for the grace to follow their example.

> Against all hope, Abraham in hope believed and so became the father of many nations, just as it had been said to him.
>
> (Romans 4:18)

God's desire for the harvest of nations will not be reaped by human effort or achievements, but only by God's interaction with us and intervention through us. Without God we can achieve nothing. But with Him all things are possible.

In many parts of the world an unprecedented harvest is being reaped. In Western Europe the media talks of the decline of Christianity and of divisions in the Church; it marginalizes Christians as irrelevant and treats them as a minority group. But in Latin America there is a vibrancy and spontaneity among huge numbers of believing Christians. Leaders are targeting for 500,000 new churches by 2010. In sub-Saharan Africa large numbers congregate to worship the Lord. In recent years millions of African Christians have participated in what is now a Global Day of Prayer. In China, India, Indonesia, and the Pacific Islands huge numbers of new churches have been planted and regularly participate in extraordinary prayer. Even in some Middle Eastern nations, traditionally viewed as Muslim, new churches are being planted, and ordinary people, disillusioned with life, are turning to the Lord. Some are having dreams and visions of the Lord. Many, through listening to radio or watching Christian television, are finding new life in Christ. Only in Europe, it seems, is there little evidence of a harvest being reaped.

I do not believe that God wants His glory to fill all parts of the earth except Europe. However, I *can* believe that for the time being we are being excluded because our faith is lacking. It's time to get desperate for God to work in our continent once more. We have seen how prayer was behind the fall of communism and the breaking down of the Berlin Wall. Where is the prayer for the breaking down of invisible walls that keep people away from experiencing the love of God for themselves? I am talking about the walls that we as churches and Christians erect, keeping people outside our believing communities. Where is the prayer of faith for things to change?

Consider these examples, and let your faith grow in what God can do. "24/7 boiler rooms" regularly see young people walk in and become overwhelmed by the powerful presence of God. When they leave, they do so as changed people – as His sons and daughters. A pastor in Cornwall in the southwest of England took some of his congregation to walk and pray regularly over a housing estate for a six-month period. Then a town-wide mission was held. This same church group then visited two estates – this one and another. All the "fruit" came from the one where they had been prayer walking.

Several churches working together in Reading (a large town west of London, where I used to live) targeted a notorious area which had become a dumping ground for problem families. We were running a church-planting, evangelism, and discipleship-training program at the time, and the idea was to have a team concentrate on this estate. We walked and prayed around this housing estate several times. God showed us what was going on and gave us insight about specific homes.

One day the team went to pray in some woods overlooking the estate, where they found witchcraft symbols on the trees and evidence of drug taking. They prayed cleansing prayers for that area, and against the work of the evil one. Ten days later a resident said to a team member, "We used to be scared to go into those woods, but it's OK now. Something's changed there." A church, led by a former drug addict, was started in the local community center. Local people began to come and many became Christians. Crime levels dropped 40 percent in two years, and social problems diminished. God answered prayer, a harvest was reaped, and lives were changed. If you want a harvest, then you must pray.

I have some good friends in Switzerland. One began to target those involved in drugs, and started a church for them. It is now a thriving community of believing ex-drug addicts. Another caught the vision for prayer and targeted people with New Age sympathies. He has seen many of them converted and fed into a network of cell groups associated with the church he started. Together they reach out to those who attend psychic fayres. Another targeted people in the arts world and media, and within two years had a church of 200 people representing many forms of artistic expression.

We call these kinds of churches "people group" churches. They are mostly made up of those who are defined by a similar lifestyle. There are also youth churches, churches planted for different language groups, and for folk of a distinct ethnic identity. These days, in their search for identity, many people develop friendships with those they work with. So we could have churches "in the market place" – those defined by the world of work. Some people congregate around a common felt need, such as a disability, so we could have churches for the deaf or dumb or partially sighted. I once met a lady from Indonesia who showed me pictures of her church. They were all women! She had trained a women's choir, taught them various skills, and equipped them to be witnesses. Their common identity? They were all former prostitutes!

Would your church know how to handle and disciple former prostitutes, drug addicts, criminals, and those with disabilities? Would your program be relevant to them? Have you successfully been able to integrate people from multiple language groups? We need to think much more radically about the harvest field in our planning for harvest. Harvests don't just happen. In all these examples, prayer has been the key to unlocking the door into specific groups.

Then there is the harvest force, the people of God – the ones to do the harvesting. How equipped are they? Have they been trained in prayer, in outreach, and faith sharing? Are they ready to cross barriers and overcome difficulties? When a farmer harvests his crop, he calls on every member of the family to help. They will spend long hours in bringing in the sheaves. Are they ready for the sacrifice involved? Some crops have to be harvested at just the right time for maximum yield and high quality. Do the workers know what to look for, how to handle the crop, how to prepare it for the next stage where it is really useful, and how to prevent it being wasted?

The Lord is looking for an army of growers, literally toilers and teachers ("laborers," as in Matthew 9:38 New King James Version). Jesus is still looking for a harvest – a harvest of souls who will not just provide us with encouraging statistics, but who will be effectively discipled, trained, and equipped to help change the world that they are part of. He is looking for the Church to grow.

Notes

1. Jim Montgomery, *Dawn 2000: Seven Million Churches to Go* (Highland Books, 1990).

2. For more information on the booklet, "Developing a Prayer Strategy," write to bmills@interprayer.com.

CHAPTER 9

HOUSES OF PRAYER
FOR ALL NATIONS

———————— ≈ ————————

For my house will be called
  a house of prayer for all nations.

(Isaiah 56:7; Mark 11:17)

*E*ACH OF THE FOUR GOSPEL WRITERS records the overturning of the table of the money changers. Matthew, Mark, and Luke set this in the context of the triumphal entry of Jesus into Jerusalem (see Matthew 21; Mark 11; Luke 19). But John separates it from the Palm Sunday event and in fact includes it as one of the early acts of Jesus, shortly after the first miracle of changing water into wine (see John 2:12–16). In each case Jesus showed His anger at what was going on in the temple. The Father did not want a place of worship used inappropriately and the worship of Mammon taking over!

Everyone was concentrating on trade, making money and changing it. Having secured Jewish money from the priests (only Jewish money was fit for worship), the money changers sat in the court of the Gentiles and exchanged it for Roman money (at a liberal profit for themselves). That's why Jesus said the temple court had become a "den of robbers." That the priests were also involved in corrupt practices seems obvious, judging by their response. They immediately sought for a way to kill Him – not what you would expect of priests!

The temple should have been a place of prayer, of encounter with God. And priests, above all, should have been there to encourage that. Was Jesus looking for a place where He could encounter His Father? After all, His Father had given the specification and design of the original temple to Solomon. When it was dedicated initially, the fire of God fell, and the glory of God was seen in visible form there (see 2 Chronicles 7:1). (That temple was burned by the Babylonians. Subsequently Zerubbabel rebuilt it, and Herod the Great enlarged and refurbished it, starting in 50 BC.) Two things pleased Jesus when He was there: the fact that the blind and lame people who came to Him were healed, and that the children were shouting, "Hosanna to the Son of David" (Matthew 21:14–16).

The purpose of the temple was still the same: to be a place of meeting with God. Jesus wanted it to fulfill its original purpose: to be a house of prayer for all nations – a place to which all nations would be welcome for prayer, and a place where prayer could be made for all nations. The temple in Jerusalem, however, couldn't be a place to which all nations came – although it is more so today in this age of travel. (But even that is beyond many peoples.) Today Jesus doesn't draw people towards the temple or its equivalent; He sends them out to the nations. Before His ascension His words to His disciples indicated that going to the nations was to be their commission. Repentance and forgiveness of sins was to be preached in His name to all nations, beginning at Jerusalem (Luke 24:47). They were to be witnesses there and "to the ends of the earth" (Acts 1:8).

Prayer – it's what reflects our fellowship and relationship with God. And prayer for all nations is what God wants us to engage in. Just over ten years ago God started to speak to me about the need to establish a house of prayer for all nations. Initially I assumed He wanted a physical place, and I would be involved. Then my wife, Ruth, wisely said, "Maybe God wants you to encourage others into that role." So I quietly kept before God what I saw as a fresh emphasis for the Church, and asked for wisdom about what to do.

One night God woke me up and told me to go to three places and challenge the people there to establish their centers as houses of prayer for all nations. I made appointments at these three places. The first was Ashburnham Place in Sussex, England, where at the time Brian Betts was center manager. When I arrived I was amazed to find that extensive building work was going on in the stable block to turn it into ... a center of prayer for all nations! God had already been speaking to them. In fact, unknown to me, John Bickersteth (a descendant of the Ashburnham family, after whom the estate was named) had sensed that the emphasis of the whole ministry was to be prayer. It was founded in prayer. Initially a praying community lived on site and had laid out the whole of the courtyard in front of the stable block in the form of a shield, each stone being laid by hand and by local Christians in prayer! Not long after my visit, Nicholas and Marigold Rivett-Carnac were appointed as the first coordinators of the prayer center.

The second place I was sent to was Pilgrims Hall, Brentwood, east of London. I had been there a couple of times before. At that time (in the early 1980s), I had been a council member of the Evangelical Alliance and had recently been appointed as their evangelism secretary. We were given a mandate from the council. With several others from the

Evangelical Alliance, we had gone to seek the Lord there about the future of the Alliance (EA, as it is called). There we heard God speak clearly to us that EA had to undergo a metamorphosis, changing from what it was into something else. Part of its future role had to do with a "trumpet-blowing" ministry. Thankfully, this is what eventually happened. Clive Calver was eventually appointed general secretary, and the whole shape and focus of EA changed radically.

Now, several years later, here I was staying overnight and due to meet with the whole community over breakfast. I shared with them what God had laid on my heart, only to hear them respond by saying, "God has already told us that we have to begin as a community to pray for the nations." Even now, this small community covers me in prayer as I go to the nations.

The third place was Bawtry Hall near Doncaster in the north of England. Bawtry Hall had been the headquarters of the Royal Air Force's Bomber Command in the Second World War. Today it is a missions center, with several Christian organizations making it their British base and sharing the common facilities, including the well-equipped conference center and ancillary rooms. I was due to speak at the weekly staff worship and prayer time, and then meet with the center manager. Before I opened my mouth, Steve Bell, one of the mission leaders there, said, "God has been saying to us that we have to establish a house of prayer for the nations here." I was flabbergasted! I suppose God had me go to these three places to encourage them that they were going in the right direction, and to encourage me that I was hearing His voice loud and clear!

Bawtry Hall did set aside a room for prayer, and invited someone from the area to serve as prayer coordinator. But, alas, it seemed that the churches in the area did not capture the vision for involvement in praying for the nations. Although the mission organizations themselves meet to pray for their own needs, they couldn't sustain the level of prayer necessary for the original vision to be fulfilled, without outside involvement and commitment. So the vision foundered. However, because of the way that the Lord led, I still believe it was and is His will for that place to be a center of prayer for the nations and not just a center of administration.

At the same time as this was going on, I became aware that other places were being established as centers of prayer and that other people were getting the vision for houses of prayer for the nations. Several people I know have turned a room in their own home into a prayer room in which they and some friends meet at different times in a week for prayer. So, tentatively, I and some friends started to interact with these places and people.

Some, like George and Trish Baxter in Plymouth, found that God had given them excellent facilities, with the initial financial backing of local churches. But they also found the vision hard to maintain in practice. Like many other places, the work in Plymouth was not sustainable because there was insufficient support from the churches. Other individuals developed their personal vision for such places to be established. Again, without the support and fellowship of local churches and Christians, rarely has that vision been sustainable.

We began to do some networking with the individual leaders. When he retired from Ashburnham Place, Brian Betts began to connect with these centers and, as part of his "retirement remit," to bring them together for mutual encouragement and prayer.[1]

We also formed a small committee to look at ways of communicating international needs and vision into local churches through regionally located prayer centers. Several of us met a number of times at the WEC International offices, hosted by John Mills and Patrick Johnstone (of Operation World fame). The fruit of our discussions eventually found an outlet several years later in a "prayer alert" service to Christians, churches, and praying groups, not only in Britain, but also around the world.[2]

Elsewhere in the world many nations have established twenty-four-hour prayer centers. Some, like the one in Colorado Springs, Colorado, USA, are big, with a limited amount of accommodation and the aim of offering continuous prayer. This particular place has gone through a series of advances and setbacks, reminding us that prayer is not an easy opt-out but a spiritual battleground.

Some 24/7 prayer centers are established out of an existing ministry of intercession. These seem to have the greatest chance of continuing, since the foundation is right. So prayer comes first, not the center! Probably the biggest one supporting twenty-four-hour prayer is the International House of Prayer in Kansas City, Missouri, USA, headed up by Mike Bickle. It has satellites all over the place!

I have visited prayer centers in many nations. God has been orchestrating something on a worldwide scale! The concept of prayer mountains – physical hills set apart for prayer – is one way this vision has been developed. As mentioned in Chapter 5, in Korea over 500 churches have "prayer mountains" – hills on which they have built retreat centers. The one owned by the Yoido Full Gospel Church in Seoul has been visited by folk from many nations. People are encouraged to spend their holidays there in twenty-four-hour prayer and fasting, booking a cubicle for this purpose. There are usually about a thousand people at any one time in around-the-clock prayer on this mountain.

My friend and colleague John Mulinde has established a prayer mountain on the outskirts of Kampala, Uganda. I was even privileged to be at its dedication. There, sometimes hundreds of people camp out in fairly primitive conditions to pray around the clock. And at their annual Africamp, thousands more come together to seek God, including representatives from many nations. Another brother has established a "prayer city" in Calabar, Nigeria, surrounded by 10,000 people who live in the vicinity, in order to sustain a high level of prayer there. I'm told that many other African nations also have national or regional houses of prayer. I've visited a prayer mountain in the Solomon Islands where, once a week, thousands of people gather to pray all night. At other times, every day, there is always somebody praying there.

In Europe the model seems to be to obtain a physical center for prayer and for retreat, and staff it with praying people, but make the center available for small groups or individuals to use for their own purposes. There are centers like this in many nations, and a Europe-wide network links them all together.

Christians in Indonesia have a vision to establish a "prayer tower" in 500 cities throughout their nation. As I write, over fifty cities have such a tower, not physical buildings (although one I visited was located in a multi-storey office block) but spiritual towers of twenty-four-hour prayer reaching towards heaven, with different churches being responsible for specific time slots, and involving hundreds of Christians in each. They also want to see 5 million intercessors trained, that is, an average of 10,000 per city, so as to sustain the level of prayer and commitment necessary to see breakthrough. And this is in the largest predominantly Muslim country in the world!

Over the past fifteen to twenty years we have witnessed a phenomenon – an amazing surge forward in prayer throughout the world. Why is God at this time leading so many of His children the world over to establish these praying centers? Can it be because He sees the need to turn up the spiritual temperature? When God's people pray, things happen. Nations change, the enemy is held back, the Kingdom of God advances. If the glory of God is to be revealed, then there needs to be a huge increase in believing prayer. Every expression of God's glory in Scripture is associated with an unusual level of prayer.

But there is another reason. Isaiah prophesied about it, and Jesus emphasized it. God's house is not in one place any more. His temple is made up of people from every tribe, people, nation, and language. Scripture envisages a time when people from every one of these will be gathered around the throne of God, worshipping Him (see Revelation 5:9; 7:9).

Only in the past 120 years has the gospel been spreading to every part of the world. But even today there are still unreached people groups, languages with no Scriptures yet available, and tribes without a church. There are still nations where persecution against God's children is severe. There are cities where it is hard to see a breakthrough. There are nations in hopeless disarray. There are disasters occurring with increasing regularity and severity. There are wars and bloodshed, with whole communities being wiped out.

All creation is groaning, "as in the pains of childbirth right up to the present time. Not only so, but we ourselves, who have the firstfruits of the Spirit, groan inwardly as we wait eagerly for our adoption." The Spirit Himself groans, as he intercedes with us and for us. All of creation is waiting "in eager expectation for the sons of God to be revealed" (see Romans 8:22–26 and verse 19). As we begin to enter into the anguish of this type of praying, through a depth of intercession that is possible when a critical mass of people comes together for prolonged interaction with the Father, Son, and Spirit, then we begin to experience this groaning for the fulfillment of all things. This is the agenda from heaven that is gripping God's people.

Following on from the vision for establishing these centers of prayer, the Holy Spirit is now emphasizing everywhere the call to continuous prayer. So the vision is multiplying. It is being called "a quiet revolution." Continuous prayer twenty-four hours a day and night is happening in prisons, housing settlements, among young people and old people. It is happening in some of these prayer centers. It is happening in some cities where churches cooperate to maintain a round-the-clock vigil. And it is happening in monasteries. Houses of prayer, centers for prayer, "boiler rooms" for prayer, prayer rooms, prayer towers – new names are being sought to describe this new phenomenon. The essence is the same; they are all helping to bring the people of God together from a wide variety of backgrounds to seek His face, to pray and worship, and to intercede for the transformation of all things. What is going to happen? What will be the answer from heaven?

Notes

1. See www.housesofprayer.net.

2. See www.prayer-alert.net.

CHAPTER 10

GO FOR THE NEXT GENERATION: MENTORING, FATHERING, DISCIPLING

———————— ≈ ————————

I HAVE MET MANY PEOPLE who occasionally get woken by God in the middle of the night because He wants them to pray about something urgently or He has some fresh instructions. This has happened to me many times – usually, I have noticed, when I am on holiday! Some of my friends suggest that during the rest of the year I am too busy, so the Lord can't get through to me; therefore He waits until I am on holiday. Maybe that's true! Anyway, I now take a pad of paper with me on holiday or when I'm traveling and have it available during the night for just such interventions.

One year, about ten days into my break when I was nice and relaxed and enjoying my rest time, God woke me in the middle of the night. This time it was something completely new. "Go for the young," He said. "Pass on to those who are half your age all I have taught you, so that they can go twice as far as you have gone in half the time it has taken you!"

Now, either I had very little to share and they could easily catch up, or God was giving me some understanding of what exponential growth was all about. I didn't try to work it out; I couldn't. I just had to trust that I had heard the Lord. They would go twice as far as me in half the time I had taken. Wow! There was more that He shared. Some of it was about the context in which this word needed sharing.

Shortly after I arrived back home, a couple of important things happened. Firstly, a friend of mine, Stuart Anderson, strongly advised me to start investing in those younger than myself. He even presented me with a picture of Paul with Timothy, which I have framed in my study. Secondly, I shared this word with the ministry team and some of the elders of our multi-congregational church in Reading. They caught the vision too, and as a result started to bring into the leadership of some congregations those who were in their early twenties. We brought three younger men into our leadership team, not as apprentices, but as full leaders. Each of them is now – years later – in full-time Christian ministry, serving the Lord among young people!

A few weeks later God started me thinking about doing something in-depth with a married couple, Steve and Kate. Steve was one of the younger additions to the leadership team of our congregation. A son of missionary parents, keenly involved in ministry to overseas students, Steve had for a while lived with us until his marriage to Kate. We had watched them develop since their student days. God led me to ask them if they would consider setting aside a day a week to work with me and learn more about prayer and spiritual warfare. Imagine my surprise when they said, "That's interesting. We were going to ask you if we could do just that." So they cut back their working arrangements to enable them to be free, and we gave ourselves six months as a trial. They would go with me on weekend seminar commitments, sharing in some of the teaching and taking part in some of the on-site prayer that was usually part of such weekends. Then we would debrief one another. They asked me to give them a reading list and set some assignments. Although this was not my skill, I readily obliged. I loved having them around, and much appreciated the interaction over the things of God. They challenged my theology and assumptions, so the whole experience was good for me as well as for them.

A couple of years ago I was speaking with a young Welshman called Gary. I asked him, "Who is mentoring you, Gary?" He actually thought I had said, "Who are you mentoring?" Without hesitation he gave me the name of a fourteen-year-old. Then I repeated my question. His mentor was an older man named Carl – someone who now greets me as "Dad" when we meet. Carl Brettle is one of those who is about half my age, whom God has put into the fast track of prayer and whose vision constantly amazes me. He started producing a quarterly prayer magazine which is distributed throughout the UK, and he is currently developing a "prayer TV" initiative. Here, then, was a four-generational relationship: Carl, Gary (fourteen years younger), the young man who is seven years younger than Gary, and of course me.

Didn't Paul have this in mind when writing to Timothy? He reminds him of the gift of faith gained from his family, "which first lived in your grandmother Lois and in your mother Eunice and, I am persuaded, now lives in you also" (2 Timothy 1:5) – three generations of spiritual influence! Thank God for those who have a godly heritage from their forebears. Treasure it, affirm it, thank God for it, and bless those who have blessed you with their prayers and have passed on their faith. I am so blessed by those who thank God for their parents and the godly example they have set.

Paul also refers to his own relationship with Timothy. He reminds him of the gift he had passed on through the laying on of hands (verse 6). He counsels him to keep what he had learned from him:

> Guard it with the help of the Holy Spirit who lives in us

Then he says:

> And the things you have heard me say in the presence of many witnesses entrust to reliable men who will also be qualified to teach others.
>
> (2 Timothy 2:2)

Here there were four generations: Paul, Timothy, "reliable men," and "others."

God, we say, is a tri-generational God. He is the God of Abraham, Isaac, and Jacob. His promise to Abraham was repeated to both Isaac the son and Jacob the grandson. The promise to Abraham would be fulfilled through Jacob (who nearly missed it because of the falling out with brother Esau). The Abramic promise is key; he was to be a father not only of his immediate family but also, God told him, of many nations (Genesis 17:4–6)!

> Through your offspring all nations on earth will be blessed, because you have obeyed me.
>
> (Genesis 22:18)

And in turn, that obedience, so God told Moses, would cause all the peoples on earth to "see that you are called by the name of the LORD" (Deuteronomy 28:10).

The process of equipping the next generation is not automatic. In many ways the younger generations of today have far more skills and abilities than the older ones. Technology has advanced so rapidly that it takes a fresh young mind brought up on computers and the latest technological advance to keep pace! Those of us who are "fathering" or "mentoring" the young need to ask them to teach us what they know, as well as being prepared to pass on what we know! We need to be challenged by the fresh ways they look at things.

The youth of today are regarded as the "tribal generation." Never before in history have the young of all cultures across the world been linked together as they are today. They have access to one another through computers, the internet, mobile phones and music. They have a shared value system. The educated ones speak English so can easily communicate across the previous barriers. The 24/7 Youth Prayer Movement has demonstrated how easy it is to be in touch with the rest of the world through the internet, and even with God (although I'm not sure if He has a computer!).

Millions of young people around the world regard themselves as the fatherless generation. This fatherlessness arises out of many influences. Some political systems exercise power in a form which has tended to squash all initiative and ingenuity. Under brutal dictatorships people live in perpetual fear, so the exercise of power and authority inhibits human development. Where fathers have been killed in wars, died from AIDS or been absent for various reasons, generations have been deprived of their fathers. Where boys have been inducted as soldiers in rebel armies and their sisters used as sex slaves, there is understandable revulsion at older men who used them, and resentment towards fathers who failed to protect them. Add to that the millions of examples of flawed fatherhood and the shocking abuse of children the world over, and it is no wonder we face this huge lack.

Today's younger generation are looking for spiritual fathers more than mentors. I have a friend in South Africa who reminds me that the word "mentoring" implies someone with knowledge teaching someone who hasn't. That's because *systems* of mentoring, based on Biblical principles, have been perfected, particularly from the United States. Spiritual *"fathering"*, however, implies relationship and mutual learning. When we look at the way Paul regarded Timothy, the language is all about relationship. He writes to him as "my true son in the faith" (1 Timothy 1:2) and "my dear son" (2 Timothy 1:2). He reminds him of this father–son relationship in 1 Timothy 1:18 and 2 Timothy 2:1. The way he instructs him is all reflective of this relationship. Of course, he is "mentoring" him too, but it is not heavy – it's loving.

However, in Paul's letter to Titus, although he uses the term "my true son" in 1:4, the language he uses is much more about advice and instruction in relation to his ministry, rather than about the way he should conduct himself. I would say that Paul here is being more of a mentor than a father to Titus, judging by this letter.

Another example is that of Elijah and Elisha. God appointed Elisha to accompany Elijah and to learn all that he could about being a prophet, since he was going to succeed him. He even learned about how to do the same kind of miracles! Yet for three years Elisha carried the bowl and washed Elijah's hands (2 Kings 3:11). There is no hint of a relationship until Elijah's time for transportation came. Then, as he is taken up from earth and from Elisha in a heavenly chariot, Elisha calls out, "My father! My father!" (2 Kings 2:12).

I think it is harder to be a father than a mentor. Mentoring is about sharing of expertise. Fathering is about sharing oneself! The best person to mentor a budding evangelist is a mature evangelist; a person with pastoral gifts needs to be under the jurisdiction of an experienced pastor. That's why it is important for theological and Bible-training institutes to identify the gifting of students and link them with people with the same gift-mix for a while. Mentoring relationships need not be long term. And the "mentee" may have more than one mentor. Some mentoring can be seen as educative, and in that context expectations are limited.

Over the years, I have taught a number of people about prayer or even one aspect of prayer, like prayer walking. Sometimes it has been only for a weekend. With others there has been an ongoing commitment. I used to go prayer walking with two or three individuals three mornings a week over a period of many months. At another time it would be with a few individuals, as part of a training course, and we would interact maybe for the duration of a teaching term. Reflecting on this, I would say I was mentoring them – for a period of time.

But with others there is more of a fathering relationship. Something (or *Someone*) connects us spiritually. When we meet we usually share with one another about many things in our lives – our struggles, our challenges, our health and finance, the balance and rhythm of life, our relationships with others in the Body of Christ – as well as about our ministry. I am constantly challenged by the need others have for spiritual fathering. I currently have several people on each continent who have requested a "fathering" relationship with me and, frankly, I struggle with how this can be developed in a meaningful and satisfactory way. I believe it reflects the lack of spiritual fathers the world over. Because of the nature of what these individuals are carrying spiritually, they find it difficult to relate to others nearer to them who do not have the same burden or insight. This is particularly true of certain types of intercessors and people called to a deeper level of intimacy with the Father in heaven and a commitment to prophetic prayer. These are not novices; most of them are what I would term significant leaders in their own right, but they are treading a lonely path.

In 2005 God spoke to me in the middle of the night (again), when I was ministering in India. The instructions were clear. I was to arrange a get-together for my spiritual sons and daughters over a number of days. He gave me a list of names and told me I was to invite them to Ashburnham

Place, Sussex, England (where I happen to be located) and not to charge them for being there. Fathers don't have their sons and daughters visit them and then ask them to pay! This was a big step of faith. I shared it with my wife first, and she thought it was a "God" idea.

Two months later God woke me again – this time in Romania: "You haven't done anything about getting your sons and daughters together. Why not?" I realized then how important this was to God and not just to me and those who would come. So, less than a year after God spoke to me, seventy people from twelve different nations gathered at Ashburnham Place for up to five days. Some came for the whole time, some for a day or more. Some brought their spouses and in some cases their children also. Most of them didn't know each other. So we spent time hearing each other's stories. We ministered to one another and did some fun things together. It was like a big family. I am still concerned also for those who were unable to come, although invited, and am waiting to see what God will say next! Even since then, there have been others in different nations that have asked to have a fathering relationship with me. Is this something of what God intended when He told Abraham he would be the father of many nations?

That there are so many people out there looking for such relationships begs the question. Although they each have a close relationship with the Father in heaven, why is it that there are not more in the Body of Christ who share the same kind of walk with God that these prayer and mission pioneers could easily relate to? Where are those leaders and potential fathers who are prepared to regard their relationship with God more highly than their ministry?

In recent years the Holy Spirit has been doing a new thing. He has been speaking to Christian leaders in the developing world about connecting more meaningfully with their spiritual fathers in the developed world. Actually, it's more about spiritual connectedness. When Ed Silvoso was visiting the UK for the first time, Roger Mitchell and I led a conference for leaders at Ashburnham Place, at which Ed was our guest speaker. It was quite a unique affair. We had invited many of those we knew who were non-white British residents.

Among them were some Brazilians who had been here as missionaries for several years. We asked them to share their hearts with us. Paolo Borges Jr shared how God had spoken to them about coming back to their spiritual parents (in missionary terms) to thank them for bringing the gospel to their people and to partner with them in going to the 10/40 Window nations. (The 10/40 Window consists of those nations between the tenth parallel north and the fortieth parallel north, from the west of Africa to the east of Asia.)

Paolo was pastor of a large church in Uberlandia in Central Brazil and was one of the leading apostolic figures in his nation. He and others had given up that responsibility to come and bless us, sent out and supported by their churches back home. "When we came, we were looking for our spiritual fathers," he said. "But all we found were the elder brothers!" (referring to the story of the prodigal's return). In other words, what they found was criticism, coldness of spirit and a lack of welcome. One of them told me that certain churches they went to didn't know what to do with them, so they were given jobs as church caretakers! And these were people who had planted scores of churches and whose ministry God had wonderfully blessed!

There are many more like that in the UK and other European nations, from all over the world – people who have been sent here by God but who are largely ignored by our leaders. What brings them here? They are looking for an ongoing relationship with those they regard as responsible for the rich spiritual heritage they now enjoy, and they want to bring blessing back to us in our so-called "post-Christian state." What keeps us from welcoming them, blessing both them and what God has done in and through them? Is it not our own pride and fear, and even jealousy that they have done better than we have? I believe we need all the help we can get to bring about a change in this "unrevived" continent, Europe. We need to welcome our spiritual sons and daughters from Latin America, the Caribbean, Africa and Asia, and the South Pacific, as well as those from the more Westernized nations.

The trouble is that many of us are not secure in our relationship with our heavenly Father and with our identity in our callings, so we are easily threatened by the success of others. Natural sons and daughters who have been away from home, and have done well at university, need to hear from their parents a resounding "Well done!" So, too, do those who have planted hundreds of churches and reached out across many barriers in what were once regarded as "missionary nations." We need to realize that many of these will do far better than we have done, and will go further than we have. They will succeed where we have failed. Is that a crime? We need to thank God for their vision, ingenuity, ability, zeal, devotion to the Lord and His Word, radical discipleship, and commitment to bringing in the Kingdom of God in their generation. We need to cheer them on, love them for who they are in God, and pray for them.

CHAPTER 11

GET INTO EUROPE

*H*AVE YOU EVER WONDERED why "the Spirit of Jesus would not allow" Paul and his companions to enter Bithynia (Acts 16:7)? He had been traveling throughout Asia, but this is the only place where we find Paul being restrained. We would say, "He had a check in his spirit." Surely the gospel was intended for them as well? Was it not the right time? Did God have some foreknowledge of danger waiting if he did go then? Or were there Christians there already (see 1 Peter 1:1)? Whatever the reason, God had other plans for Paul.

He went on to Troas, a port on the Aegean Sea – the gateway to Europe. That night he had a vision: a man from Macedonia "standing and begging him" to come over and help (Acts 16:8). It was his first visit to Troas; he had only just arrived, yet here he was immediately making preparations to go. His companions, including Doctor Luke, witnessed that God was calling them to preach the gospel there. The rest, as they say, is history!

There was no time to check things out with those who had witnessed their original call in Antioch, or with the Council in Jerusalem. Nobody had done a reconnaissance trip. They had to follow the Spirit's promptings. The same

Spirit who had stopped them going to Bithynia was now opening the door for them to new pastures. People who do the same kind of thing today we describe as "having a free spirit," which by implication suggests that they are unreliable and unpredictable. "But this was Paul, the apostle," you say. "But this was the Spirit of God," I say.

How many missionaries or servants of God have we heard say, "God led me to go there," or "God told me to do that," or "God opened the door here," or "God closed the door there"? The same God who directed the steps of St Paul wants to direct our steps also.

> Since we live by the Spirit, let us keep in step with the Spirit.
> (Galatians 5:25)

"Oh, that's all right for Paul," some suggest. "He was special. Besides, it was a different era; it was the early Church in action, and it was a different culture then." Oh, yes? Then why is God speaking so frequently to so many of His servants today to go and do things they have never done before, never thought of doing, and wouldn't possibly have attempted without God instructing them?

Being prepared to hear the voice of God means I am willing to place myself utterly at His disposal, do what He wants, follow His leading, and attempt the impossible, if that is what He asks and says is necessary. Living a life of faith implies a willingness to entrust the next step to God, whatever that might mean. It might also mean God saying, "I know you love me and your heart is right. I don't want you to go anywhere. I just want you to love those around you and be willing to hear my voice on a day-to-day basis. I want to entrust some errands to you. Just walk with me and we will do some exploits in your town!"

It isn't a question of geography. It's a matter of obedience – and of fellowship with God. I love hearing how God has led His servants to do things "outside the box." I love it when God takes ordinary people, doing ordinary things, and entrusts them with a little bit of His extraordinary agenda! I have so many names flooding through my mind as I write that I wish I could tell you their stories. Stories of changes in their community, of schools being transformed, of drug-running cartels being "busted," of dramatic healings, of people with their own actual visions from heaven, of angelic appearances, of people being in the right place at the right time. Stories of God waking people to pray in order to avert catastrophic disasters. Nation changers! World changers! People who, against hope, believed. People who brought heaven to earth for some person or tribe. People who sacrificed home, career, marriage prospects, and financial security to serve the King of kings, and to go anywhere, do anything, and be anything He wanted, for the sake of knowing that they were doing His will. But it's much better that you hear their stories straight from their mouths – that's part of what eternity is for!

St Paul was one of those! And we in Europe became the cradle of Christianity. For 2,000 years the gospel has been preached in this continent, and from this continent has been exported to every part of the world. We have an amazingly rich heritage. Two thousand years of Christianity! Two thousand years of serving the one true God. However, what Paul brought us and taught us needs to be rediscovered again. We need some more "Pauls" from around the world to come over with that same kind of "Spirit of Jesus" and show us what it means to trust in God day by day.

I had been focused almost entirely on the British Isles. For a while, it was merely Britain. Then God sovereignly led me to be involved in Northern Ireland, which I began to visit two or three times a year for prayer-related ministry. This was during the period of continuing terrorism. Often God had me go there at crucial times, when the latest and most significant atrocity occurred, or times when bombs went off in the same place that I had prayed the day before! I visited some of the top-security prisons, and met and prayed with those who had become Christians inside – previous enemies now reconciled and praying with and for one another. There were many supernatural "coincidences," when God's timing was obvious. I used to refer to Northern Ireland as our "back door," and say that we shouldn't be praying for other places and situations without praying for Ireland. All this preceded the "peace process" that the British and Irish governments have been pursuing for several years. I believe that winning the spiritual battle first contributed to the many changes that have occurred there. There's more about this in a later chapter.

Then suddenly the "Macedonian call" came. The Lord said, "Get into Europe! Build bridges of relationship in Europe and prepare the way for others to follow you." When God speaks, He usually has ways of confirming His word. I was at the beginning of involvement with what became the European Prayer Link, a ministry to link leaders of prayer across Europe. Together with Johannes Facius, Pieter Bos, and Rick Ridings, we had begun to meet and pray and plan.

Cindy Jacobs was visiting London from the United States, I think for the first time. We were both speakers at a conference at St Mark's, Kennington, London, which was being facilitated by Julie Anderson. I had just finished speaking, and joined with Cindy, her husband Mike, and Julie in a small prayer group. Cindy started praying over me, saying that God wanted me in Europe, and had special links in Brussels, Amsterdam, southern Germany, and especially Switzerland. Cindy knew nothing of what God had been saying to me. Nor to my knowledge did she know the other three. But Rick Ridings lived in Brussels, Pieter Bos in Amsterdam, and Johannes Facius in southern Germany. And I had just received my first invitation for ministry in Switzerland!

Shortly afterwards, I was asked if I could be involved in helping to develop prayer in relation to church planting across Europe through DAWN. Then, suddenly, the doors opened wide and throughout the 1990s invitations to various European countries and events poured in, and involvement with those with a heart to see things change in Europe proliferated. In fact many times I was unable to respond to invitations as there were so many of them. But if they were strategic I suggested others to go in my place – people like Rachel Hickson and Faith Forster, among others.

A strong relationship was developed with Uli Haldemann, a Swiss leader who became one of the leaders within the prayer movement in his nation, and is committed to seeing his nation transformed and offered back to God. Uli opened the door for me to do a prayer-teaching tour of Swiss cities, and he translated "Developing a Prayer Strategy" into Swiss German. Later, others invited me to share among all the city-based Evangelical Alliances about prayer. And many times I've been up on the mountains to pray! Some of the most significant events I've been involved with in recent years have also been held in Switzerland. Today, every village community in Switzerland (over 2,500 of them) has a prayer group praying for it, that God would visit and bring change to its people.

I met Wolfgang Simson through my DAWN connections, and we were both part of the DAWN Europa team, strategizing, training, and seeking to facilitate church-planting movements across Europe. He and I did several meetings together – in Switzerland! At one of them God started speaking to me about the Nazi gold locked up in Swiss banks. Once that started to be returned to its rightful owners, God would open Switzerland to be become a spiritual blessing to the nations, as the rivers that flow from their land already blessed the rest of Europe. More recently Chris and Chipi Daza, who lead prophetic prayer schools in Switzerland, have become linked with us. The nation I have visited the most has been Switzerland. And none of this have I engineered!

We (that is, the European Prayer Link) held prayer conferences in nearly every nation in Europe over a ten-year period, including those just emerging out of the trauma of communism. When God said, "Get into Europe," I could not have known that the Berlin Wall was to come down less than two years later! God removes all barriers when He is on the move. John and Yvonne Pressdee, who pioneered long-distance prayer walking (now called "prayer expeditions"), invited me to join them in the London to Berlin and the Berlin to Moscow prayer expeditions. These were immensely significant, where we all saw God at work in extraordinary ways through prayer. With others I have prayer walked in dozens of European cities.

Through the Evangelical Alliance, we launched specific prayer calls on European issues, such as the Bosnian War, the European Union, and the needs of Eastern bloc nations. My colleague, David Sladden, used to accompany me on many of these journeys, and from it God began to develop His plans for David's life. David is now writing his first book on the spiritual history of Europe, something which I believe will be important for church leaders for decades to come.

Under the auspices of the European Prayer Link we held what we patronizingly called a "mentoring conference" and invited a number of "younger" prayer leaders to share the time with us in Vallence, France. It was not a huge success! However, lasting friendships were formed, and some of these younger leaders became part of the European prayer leadership. From that developed the Connect Europe youth prayer movement, facilitated by Marc van der Woude, a tall Dutchman.

Onto the scene stepped Amaury Braga, one of the Brazilian missionaries referred to in the previous chapter.

He had a vision to bring some Brazilian pastors and inter-cessors to the United Kingdom; initially it was for about thirty to fifty people. Then the vision grew. So, in 1997 we ended up with 180 pastors and intercessors, from many parts of Brazil, arriving at five separate London airports on the same day. We met them with coaches and transported them to a conference in Lancashire, hosted by the Brazilian missionary group, Go to the Nations. From there they split into five groups and went to the capital cities of the British Isles and Ireland: London, Edinburgh, Cardiff, Belfast, and Dublin. For five days Christians hosted them, introduced them to their cities and country, and received their prayers, love, and ministry. Then they all came back to London and from there dispersed to eleven European cities in eleven different countries.

It was a logistical nightmare! Without the help of Russell Baylis, a pastor/teacher from Reading, we wouldn't have achieved it. It was significant, not only for those involved, but also because of the ongoing relationships that some cities have established with their Brazilian visitors. Go to the Nations ministry has since established partnerships with churches in many of the countries visited, and ongoing connections have been made with some 10/40 Window nations as an outcome. Independently of me, my friend Roger Mitchell also caught the vision for Europe, by launch-ing Target Europe, an attempt to get the Church around the world focused on the 40/70 Window (those nations from the fortieth parallel north to the seventieth parallel north – that is, all of Europe from the west of Ireland and Portugal to the Ural Mountains). For five years from the year 2000 he mobilized a new army of prophetic, praying people for a new century. From this has developed a "night-watch" for Europe in which intercessors from many nations commit an hour a night on a regular basis to be in prayer for European needs and issues.

When God told me to "Get into Europe," none of this was in prospect. Although God has since moved me on to the rest of the world, I still retain a longing to see Europe change, and what has been termed a "post-Christian" continent become open to God in a powerful new way. However, I also know that this isn't just for me to respond to!

Europe has been variously described as the "unrevived continent," the "post-Christian West," and the biggest "Jewish graveyard" in the world. Today its religion is secularism and football. Millions indulge in the worship of their football team every week, whilst many historic churches lie almost empty with few worshippers and crumbling buildings. Two world wars in the twentieth century left millions dead as European countries fought each other. Religious divides, existing over many centuries, have also ended in bloody conflicts. This is a blood-stained continent, and blood cries out from the land, which needs healing. The promise of 2 Chronicles 7:14 is relevant for us, when God said, "I ... will heal their land." So, for Europe, transformation is not merely about the transforming of individuals; it is also about the transforming of relationships, of communities deeply divided; about the need for national repentance and forgiveness, which involves us turning from wickedness, praying, and returning to God; and it is about the healing of the land – this continent.

The ending of communism and the breaking down of the Berlin Wall in 1989 were huge answers to prayer. We had hoped this would usher in a new period of rapid church growth in Eastern Europe. But instead, into the vacuum left by a failed communist system came hoards of New Age practitioners and the materialism that had overtaken the West. The DAWN movement has for more than fifteen years been trying to get sustainable church-planting movements going, throughout the whole of Europe. Whilst there has been some notable progress, particularly in Eastern countries such as Ukraine and Romania, there is still a very long way to go.

Europe was the first continent to be evangelized by the early Church and became the cradle of Christianity. The era of modern missions was birthed from us. Today it needs to be re-evangelized. I describe Europe as a "tired old man," the best years having passed. What we need is the love and attention of our children. But like an independent, widowed grandfather, we tend to thrust away from us the very people we need to help us! God has His servants in every country and is bringing from every country of the world those with a burden to contribute their bit in the re-evangelization of Europe. He is calling hundreds of people from the nations that, in the past, European missionaries helped evangelize. He is telling them to go back to bless the countries of their spiritual forebears. It really is a new day.

I wonder if, when Paul responded to his Macedonian call, he had any idea as to where it would lead and what would transpire. In a few short years he only managed to get to Greece, Malta, Cyprus, Italy, and Croatia (Illyricum in Scripture – see Romans 15:19). But he paved the way for others. He wasn't the only one to bring the gospel to Europe. Some of the Roman slaves who were transported across the nations, even as far as Britain, were Christians. And, I wonder, did the Gauls and Celts, who lived in parts of Asia Minor and were part of the church in Galatia, imbibe some of Paul's missionary spirit? So that, when they migrated through North Africa and up the western coast of France and Ireland, they brought the gospel with them? History tells us that this happened.

Paul was a pioneer, a truly apostolic person. His whole life was shaped by his relationship with God. Like many of the patriarchs and prophets of old, he had a very personal connection with heaven. His conversion was as a result of a personal encounter with the risen Christ. The blindness that ensued was ended when, in prayer, he had a vision of Ananias coming to him.

When the Holy Spirit caused Barnabas and him to be set apart for missionary work (see Acts 13:1–3), this was another stage in a spiritual journey of obedience and walking with God. So what happened in Troas was part of his ongoing experience of God's supernatural intervention in his life and leading. Professor F.F. Bruce in his writings referred to Paul as "the Apostle of the free spirit." Would that we were all like Paul! Free to be led by the Spirit, free in doing what He says, and freely able to perceive the Spirit's leading.

CHAPTER 12

PREPARING FOR REVIVAL

———————≈———————

REVIVAL! THE WORD CONJURES UP IMAGES (if you are an avid reader of revival literature, as I am) of God's supernatural intervention in church and society. Students of the history of revivals will recall the way it used to happen, of tales of earnest seeking after God by saint and sinner alike, of large numbers of people coming together to hear God's word, of rapid church growth, and of supernatural manifestations. But in recent years I have noticed that the word is being used less and less in Western Christian circles.

Now it is "transformation" – transformation of the individual, church, society, community, and nation! To a large extent this desire has been fed by the outstanding series of videos produced by George Otis Jr of the American-based Sentinel Group, plotting stories of transformation around the world. But on taking a closer look, one recognizes similar evidences to those of historic revivals!

Many Western Christians have prayed for revival for years. But alas, that prayer in the twenty-first century seems to have lapsed. Why? Many have stopped praying because they think that God doesn't want to bring revival to their nation, or that their nation deserves the judgment of God more than His mercy. Some have fasted and prayed much, but have seen little or no response from heaven. It's as if some expect their prayers to be instantly answered, or that if we do the right things, God is bound to answer. Having heard of what God seems to be doing in parts of the so-called developing world, and faced with no evidence of similar things happening in Western nations, they have naturally become disillusioned. Has God given up on us? Or have we given up on God?

Some leaders have even suggested that praying for revival should not even be on our agenda. They suggest that as revival is a supernatural sovereign work of God, and happens only rarely in history, it is futile for us to spend much time praying for it. God will do it in His own way, in His own time, and nothing we can do or not do will alter that. Some have been influenced by apparent prophetic words that revival was going to occur in a certain year, but when that year passed without any change, they gave up praying and looking for it.

Having been in situations in different parts of the world where all the classic evidences of revival are to be seen, I know that God has not left this world's scene in despair. Having seen how the prayers of God's people have, from our human perspective, been such a key element in preparing the way, I know that God is still answering the burdened, impassioned pleas of His children. And having met people whose lives have been profoundly touched and who live on a different level of relationship with God than most in our postmodern Westernized culture, it leaves me with a longing for more and more people to experience the same.

The testimony of people like John Wesley, George Whitefield, Jonathan Edwards, William Haslam, Billy Bray, and Evan Roberts still echo down through the last three centuries. The experiences of the "awakenings" of the eighteenth and nineteenth centuries provide us with a historical backcloth that we should neither ignore nor forget.

Some years ago, my own desires after God were influenced greatly by revival literature and by conferences examining the key elements. My mentor in those days was the late Dr Edwin Orr. An Irishman by birth, he used to cycle around the villages of Ireland preaching the gospel. With a heart for evangelism, he had gone to live in the United States, from whence he made several trips into Latin America. He was part of a prayer group which included Billy Graham (the international evangelist) and Bill Bright (founder of Campus Crusade for Christ). He became an ardent student of revivals and a researcher into revivals. In his day he was a legendary authority on "spiritual awakenings," as he preferred to call them. He used to lead annual study conferences in Oxford on "Revival," and was a member of the faculty of the Board for World Mission at Fuller Seminary in Pasadena, California.

His own understanding of revivals was shaped by history. He distinguished between "revival," which he saw as the reviving of the saints, and an "awakening," which he saw as the movement of large numbers of uninstructed people towards faith in Christ – not through evangelism only, but also through the dynamic activity of the Holy Spirit. In Europe, we would equate "renewal" with his definition of revival, and point to the renewing work of the Holy Spirit experienced by tens of thousands in many nations during the Charismatic Renewal of the 1970s and 1980s and in the so-called Toronto Blessing of the 1990s.

Edwin Orr kept alive my own interest in revival and awakening. When he stayed with my wife and me, or when I journeyed with him, he used to ply me with stories of his latest research and of how God had worked in the past. His keen sense of humor used to liven up any conversation. I took him once to a national conference of the Lydia

Fellowship International in Derbyshire. Collecting him afterwards, I asked, "How was it"?

"Ever been a lion in a den of Daniels?" he quipped.

It was his influence on my life that led to my appointment by the Evangelical Alliance as their first "prayer and revival secretary." I suppose the fact that I didn't oversee a revival in Britain caused the word "revival" to be dropped in the job specification of my successors! It really did create expectations that were not in my power to fulfill! However, I did carry a burden (and still do) to see the supernatural power of God poured out and large numbers of my fellow countrymen turn to the Lord.

Tom Houston, former general director of the Bible Society, and a friend of many years, once asked me, "What would you love to see by the end of the twentieth century?"

Immediately I replied, "I would love to see this nation experience revival, and to be alive to see it."

The twentieth century has been and gone, and we haven't seen a revival (or spiritual awakening) in any part of Europe, to my knowledge, in the last fifty years. I call Europe the "unrevived continent." But I still cherish a desire to see God move supernaturally in bringing large numbers into relationship with Him, whatever the terminology we happen to use.

So how do we prepare for revival? I wrote a book on this topic in 1988. In 2004 this was published in Korean, which is interesting. Ten years earlier the Church around the world would have regarded what was happening in the Korean church as revival. The phenomenal church growth, the huge prayer meetings, and the size of the churches provided many of us Westerners with challenges to see something similar in our own countries. In the mid-1990s ten of the twenty largest churches in the world were located in Korea. I have met several of the pastors of these large churches, and visited the Yoido Full Gospel Church in Seoul, the capital of

Korea, a couple of times. The church seats 25,000 people, and there are overflow rooms able to seat another 15,000. Seven services are held each Sunday, and several others on other days of the week. There are scores of satellite congregations in the suburbs. Hundreds pray around the clock on their prayer mountain.

Over 4,000 leaders were hosted by the Hallelujah Church in Seoul at an International AD 2000 Consultation in 1995. We were guests at a stadium rally when 80,000 young people dedicated themselves to world mission. One meets these Koreans all over the world today, and several I have spoken with were present at that rally! Prayer meetings of over 2 million people have been held in the Yoido Plaza in Seoul. Yet the Koreans do not think they are in "revival." In recent years this phenomenal church growth has not, I understand, been maintained. The materialism of the West has influenced the lifestyle of Korea's people as the Pacific-rim nations began to experience economic growth. So maybe they are asking the same kind of questions as Western nations. Why has church growth tailed off?

Meanwhile, the Church around the world has turned its attention elsewhere. We are all anxious to learn what we can from the spiritual wells that God has opened up in other places. So thousands of leaders make pilgrimages to huge successful churches elsewhere or to nations where phenomenal breakthroughs have been seen. No longer does Korea have the monopoly on large churches or huge prayer meetings. Many other nations have also seen extraordinary manifestations of God's favor.

Places where spiritual wells have been opened up in the past still retain something of the original stream of blessing. Physical wells can become blocked or poisoned, so preventing the purpose for which they were created from being fulfilled. When the Philistines blocked the wells that Abraham had dug, Isaac had to come along later and reopen them. Then he also dug new wells (see Genesis 26:15–33). This phase of re-digging the wells must have caused a great deal of joy. Centuries later, Jesus met a woman by one of Jacob's wells, and through that encounter many Samaritans believed (John 4:5–6, 39). As far as we know, Jacob didn't discover or dig any new wells. But he did inherit what his forebears had founded, and bought land from Hamor, and it became known as "Jacob's well" (see Genesis 33:19; John 4:6)! What did he do? He built an altar to the Lord there!

Ron belonged to an American Brethren congregation. He was one of those on a Revival Wells tour, led by my friend Bryan Pullinger, for a group of Americans who were in the United Kingdom to connect with some of their spiritual roots. They visited Loughor in South Wales, where the 1904–05 Welsh Revival began. I would say that was a revival well! As they were walking along the street towards Moriah Chapel, Ron collapsed into a bush, weeping. There he met with God in a new way, as thousands had done nearly a hundred years before him. The same group visited Lindisfarne in Northumbria and spent a night on this "sacred" island. Like many before them, they too had an extraordinary experience of God whilst there.

Herrnhut in Germany is another such well. Here in 1727 the outpouring of God on the Moravian church kickstarted a 100-year-long prayer meeting. And here, through an encounter with God, a young man called Pete Greig began the contemporary 24/7 Youth Prayer Movement. Where are the other spiritual wells in our European nations where, in the past, the blessing of God has been experienced? Let's find out what caused the flow of blessing to be stemmed, do some repenting, and ask God to reopen these wells once more.

So what can we learn from elsewhere, in time and distance? God's promises do not fail. God's Word is still relevant. And if we do what He says, He hears our prayer.

Extraordinary prayer, holiness of life, repentance and reconciliation, unity, and love for God and one another – this is,
was, and will always be God's recipe. However, God is the
Master of timing; we are not. He will choose His moments
of breakthrough.

2 Chronicles 7:14 is still the verse above all that the Holy
Spirit is emphasizing. God spoke to Solomon these words:

> If my people, who are called by my name, will *humble them-
> selves* and *pray* and *seek my face* and *turn from their wicked ways*,
> then will I hear from heaven and will forgive their sin and will
> heal their land.
>
> (2 Chronicles 7:14, emphasis added)

Every phrase is pregnant with meaning. Although this word
from the Lord applied specifically to Israel, it was not exclu-
sive to them. The principle applies to the children of God of
any generation and in every nation. It is still God's promise,
in response to Solomon's prayer of dedication of a well of
blessing – the temple. Five times in his prayer, Solomon asks
God, if the people pray, then "hear from heaven and forgive
the sin of your people" (2 Chronicles 6:21, 25, 27, 30, 39).

"If my people will humble themselves"

Nobody finds that humility comes naturally. "Sorry" is
the hardest word to say, apparently. We don't humble ourselves in order to pray; rather, we need to humble ourselves
because we are proud, arrogant, bumptious, self-opinion-
ated, self-promoting, self-reliant, self-righteous, self-seeking,
and self-everything-else.

> God opposes the proud,
>   but gives grace to the humble.
>
> (Proverbs 3:34; James 4:6)

That should make us say "Ouch!" We need to humble ourselves over many things, many acts, and many relationships where self has been allowed to predominate and dominate. We also need to humble ourselves before God over our persistence in thinking we can do His work in our way, promote His Kingdom with our ideas and methods, and over our stubborn refusal to acknowledge that we have failed.

"If my people will pray"

Prayer is multi-faceted. And prayer can take place in many ways. Prayer is not just what we do; it's who we are. Prayers are not merely said in Sunday services; they are the bread and butter of our relationship with our Father in heaven – day by day, hour by hour, and minute by minute. However, few know much about the depth of prayer that is necessary and possible. When one sees the travail that characterizes the prayers of God's children elsewhere, and the hours spent in intercession over big issues, Western Christians have a lot to learn. And when we begin to understand Biblically the prophetic prayer that characterized the way that Abraham, Moses, David, Daniel, Nehemiah, Ezra, Ezekiel, Jeremiah, and many others interceded about situations to which they had no human answer, then we will begin to see that our prayers too can make a difference.

Every revival in history has been preceded by and accompanied by what is termed "extraordinary prayer"! We use another term, "revival praying," to try and define this type of prayer. It is prolonged (sometimes lasting many days), sacrificial (involving going without food or sleep), earnest, desperate, and divinely generated (when somehow human desire and divine unction connect). It is prayer that is full of faith, is characterized by a new level of holiness and awareness of sin, and involves an experience of the tangible presence of God.

"If my people seek my face"

In the West we seek God's hand, not His face. We are interested in what He can do. But God looks for us to seek His face; He wants us to know Him and what He is like. King David prayed:

> One thing I ask of the LORD,
>   this is what I seek:
> that I may dwell in the house of the LORD
>   all the days of my life,
> to gaze upon the beauty of the LORD
>   and to seek him in his temple.
>
> (Psalm 27:4)

It's worthwhile for us to pray that too.

> My heart says of you, "Seek his face!"
>   Your face, LORD, I will seek.
>
> (Psalm 27:8)

A friend said to me once, "Brian, don't seek God for revival. Seek Him for Himself." Good advice. Intimacy with the Father should be a priority for us. That intimacy is elusive in a busy, materialistic way of life. Yet it is something God is constantly beckoning us into. If we seek His face, and spend time in His presence, then it is His presence that we will carry with us. We will become modern-day equivalents of Moses and Joshua whose faces shone as a result of spending time in the presence of God (see Exodus 33 and 34).

"If my people turn from their wicked ways"

This should be applied individually and corporately. All the instances that I am aware of around the world where God is breaking through are associated with public confession

of sin on behalf of ourselves, both individually and corporately, and on behalf of our forebears. So many sins of
the past have been ignored. We have pretended that we
could get away with murder – literally. But God abhors the
shedding of innocent blood (Habakkuk 2:8, 12, 17; Isaiah
59:1–3), even that which is hundreds of years old (Matthew
23:30, 35). He dislikes disunity (see Isaiah 58:3–4). He wants
unity among His people (John 13:34–35) and oneness with
Himself (John 17:20–21). He wants a holiness in us that is
like His, so that any blemish of character is immediately
repented of and cleansed, enabling us to show the world a
different way to live. Without that, our message has a hol-
low ring about it. Turning from our wicked ways requires
a repentant heart, a readiness to acknowledge our wickedness, and a willingness to turn from all things that God may
point out as being wicked, unholy, and inappropriate for
seekers after God. Then, God says ...

"I will hear from heaven, forgive your sin, and heal your land"

The Christians in Fiji have found, since 2003, that this literally happens. When they do the praying, the humbling of
themselves, and the turning from their sins, God not only
forgives their sin but He literally heals their land – even
within twenty-four hours! The blood-stained land is healed.
The unforgiven sin is forgiven. Repentance and reconciliation occurs. The spirits of men, women, and children, who
have been unjustly killed, are set free. Covenants made with
witchcraft, idolatry, and with the land are repented of and
renounced. Addictions are brought to an end. Communal
deliverance takes place. Infertile land recovers its fertility.
Poisoned waters are made pure. Dead coral comes back
to life. And nature produces an abundance on land and in
the sea.

When we consider the gross sins committed in our Western liberal culture that offend God and His holy character; when we factor in the shedding of innocent blood across the so-called Christian continent of Europe during the wars of the twentieth century; when we realize the huge number of innocents killed in the wombs of women over the past fifty years; when we as God's children start to realize the connection we have with land and history; when we start to take sin seriously, and God's Word seriously, then maybe we shall see Him fulfill His promise in His Word. And when we repent of the bloodshed caused by the Church in the religious wars of the seventeenth century, as we have done over the blood shed during the Crusades of the tenth and eleventh centuries, and deal with the legacy of colonial injustices around the world, the appalling legacy of slavery, and the complicity of Christians and the Church in this – then, maybe then, we shall be able to ask God to forgive our sin and heal our land.

It's time to prepare for revival! We are not there yet. But it is time to get ready. How desperate are we for God to work in our nation, and in the hard places on this globe? How desperate are we for His presence, His glory, and His character? The answers to those questions will determine whether we are ready. God will, when we will. He will answer when we do what 2 Chronicles 7:14 says we need to do.

CHAPTER 13

PRINCIPALITIES AND POWERS OVER NATIONS

—————————— ≋ ——————————

*I*N CHAPTER 7 WE DISCUSSED SPIRITUAL WARFARE over our cities, and the way that the character of a city can be shaped by the spiritual powers invoked over it by its citizens. If that is true of cities, it is also true of nations.

My friend Pieter Bos has written a major work entitled *The Nations Called*,[1] which in some ways develops the theme of the redemptive calling assigned to individual nations. I cannot hope to deal as thoroughly as he does with such a big subject, nor with the reasoning that led to his conclusion. In this chapter, however, I want to share what I have sensed, as I have visited various nations, about the spiritual powers that seem to be at work there, and how and why.

Are there such things as principalities and powers over nations? Biblically, yes! But in practice do we recognize this and do something about it? The answer, unfortunately, is a resounding (or maybe a weak) "No!". The question is, Why not?

According to Romans 8:38 and Ephesians 6:10–12, there are "principalities" and "powers" (Authorized Version), or "rulers" and "authorities" (NIV) – and demons – operating in this "dark world." Paul also asserts that we are up against "spiritual forces of evil in the heavenly realms." If they are at work in this world, where are they, who are they, and how do they operate? What is their connection with the heavenly realms? And what responsibility do we have against them? Does "this dark world" refer only to *physical* earthly rulers and authorities, like governments, or is there instead (or also) a *spiritual* dimension behind this? In that Paul is writing about the opposition in the spiritual war as being not of "flesh and blood," we can deduce that there has to be a spiritual interpretation to his words. Paul also asserts that Christ "is the Head over every power and authority" and that He "disarmed the powers and authorities ... triumphing over them by the cross" (Colossians 2:10, 15). So they are disarmed, but not done away!

In Daniel 10 we read of Daniel being in a period of prayer and partial fasting for twenty-one days. At the end of this time he learns that, unknown to him and beyond his sight, an intense battle had been going on between the angel from God and the spiritual custodian over the nation of Persia, referred to as "the prince." Only when reinforcements came in the person of Daniel's angel (verse 21), who was no less than Michael, referred to as "one of the chief princes" (verse 13), was the breakthrough possible. A "prince" in this context is surely someone belonging to the "principalities and powers." A principality is a territory over which a prince is leader. The angel also referred to the "prince of Greece," whom he would also face during his return journey to his heavenly home. Where did this battle take place? In context, it didn't happen on earth – it must have occurred in "the heavenly realms."

Daniel physically was in the nation of Babylon at the time, not far from what is now Baghdad. Actually, he was standing on the banks of the River Tigris, which flows through modern-day Iraq. Babylon had conquered Israel and the Jews, and led many into captivity. It had then been subsumed into the bigger entity, the Medo-Persian Empire under Cyrus (or Darius) (see Daniel 5:31). This empire was huge, encompassing 1 million square miles of territory, stretching from the River Tigris in the west to the River Indus in the east (in modern-day Pakistan). It lasted from 539 to 331 BC. So the "principality" of Persia had a large physical territory over which he had jurisdiction, and presumably had, in the heavenly realms, the prince of Babylon as one of his underlings.

All of this tells us that there is a spiritual realm where a power struggle is perpetually occurring, but which also involves earthly situations. Actual nations have heavenly princes over them. What we don't know is what they do, and how their power is expressed. We know that there is a system of fallen angels and evil spirits that are always at work. But we can deduce from the way they interact with earth what kind of strongholds of power they build, and we can learn from experience how that power holds people in bondage. I have learned from those who once were heavily involved in witchcraft that in their past they were in league with such demonic principalities, had been taught a foreign language by demons, and used to astral-travel to the territory over which they had joint responsibility. Fortunately, those I know are now committed to advancing the Kingdom of God!

I have noticed, during the many visits I have made to Northern Ireland and to the Republic of Ireland, that there is a spiritual difference once you cross the physical border. The South seems to be much more spiritually "open" than the North. In the North, one is reminded all the time of the conflict lying beneath the surface and the entrenched attitudes that hold people in positions of allegiance to one side or the other. Various areas of the land (villages, towns, even streets) had been marked out as either Republican or Loyalist territory. People raise their flags and even paint the pavements to show under whose territorial influence you happen to be. Try moving from one to the other in a prayerful way, and you immediately pick up the tension and the difference in the "spiritual atmosphere." I have also noticed that many Northern Irish inhabitants who move away from their own land to somewhere else in the world lose this fierce sense of loyalty and begin instead to see their own nation and the island of Ireland in a completely different light. I would say that by coming out from under the influence of the prevailing powers, be they physical or spiritual or both, they become open to a completely different "spirit."

Spring Harvest, an annual Christian event held over the weeks of Easter each year in various locations around Britain, were having a focus on Europe at each of their weeks in 1989. At the time, 10,000 people were at each week's event – an aggregate of over 70,000 for each Easter. I was the prayer coordinator for the week. At each of the venues, we were focusing on prayer for Europe at one of the evening celebrations. We had flags for every nation of Europe, to provide a visual focus for our prayers. There was one flag missing – for the nation of Albania. "Brian, would you lead us in prayer at the end for Albania?" the event leadership team asked.

Albania was ruled by a rigid communist dictator who, a couple of years earlier, had declared Albania to be the world's first (and only) atheistic state. Albania was predominantly Muslim in culture and there were no known Christians and certainly no known church there. The communist system still held all of Eastern Europe in its iron grip. To my shame I had never before prayed for Albania. So I said to God, "Help! What do I pray for Albania?"

The Lord was wonderful! Back came His promptings: "You see Albania as like a hard-boiled egg; I see it as an egg with life in it that is about to burst forth."

We all had mini-maps of Europe printed on a sheet of paper. I asked the thousands present to lay a finger on the nation of Albania (it was finger-sized on the map) and join me in prayer as I prayed in faith with what God had told me.

In November that year (eight months later) the communist system began to collapse and the Berlin Wall began to be demolished. The previously inconceivable had happened. The dictator of Albania was deposed and lost his life. A couple of years later, at one of our European conferences, I shared a room with an Albanian Christian, called Pellumb Kllogjeri. He had come to the Lord in 1990. Since then he had spent hours each day in studying the Bible and in prayer; he had a lot to catch up on, he told me! From then on, we helped Pellumb to come to as many European prayer gatherings as he could. He is an outstanding Christian and today is president of his nation's Evangelical Alliance. Despite the nation going through civil unrest since, and being one of the poorest in Europe, nevertheless God has worked extraordinarily there. Pellumb's story is one of those you will want to hear in eternity!

Later I found out that the Lydia movement in Scotland had for years past been praying for Albania as their "adopted nation." Albania was also the only European nation included in the 10/40 Window prayer focus throughout the 1990s. And I have met others, from around the world, who had been praying for this nation. "When God intends great mercy for a people or a nation, He first of all sets us praying," said Matthew Henry.

On my first visit to Belgium, as our plane was descending to land in Brussels, I asked God, "What is Belgium like"?

Immediately came back the answer: "It is full of the Masonic."

As I was being taken by car from the airport, I asked the Christian who collected me about this.

"Don't you know?" he asked. "Brussels is a stronghold of the Masonic. The gardens between the Royal Palace and the State Parliament are laid out with Masonic symbols." And there was more than this, of course.

Why did God tell me about this? He obviously knows what it is like on planet earth and I think He waits to inform us. But He waits for us to ask Him. If we are prepared to do something about this planet, then we need to know what He knows, and we need to be forewarned about what we are entering into. Of course this is not an exact science. Our knowledge is partial, and God may not show us everything. But I believe He does communicate on a "need to know" basis. It would be an interesting exercise to explore, with others who have heard God speak about their nation, just what He has said and what we have done about it! What have I done? Each time I have been in Brussels I have been there to pray. Sometimes I have engaged in a prayer walk around many of the significant landmarks, usually with others. That is another story we will have to hear about in eternity!

On one occasion the European Prayer Link team was in Hungary to hold a prayer conference. As a leadership team we were friends, and would have said that we walked in unity. But at this conference our disunity was exposed, and we had the most difficult time in our entire experience. Why? Undoubtedly there were character factors within each of us, which later we had to confront. But also we had come into a nation that had historically been riven by division, that itself had controlled a huge Empire (the Austro-Hungarian). It had recently been under the controlling influence of communism and was just coming out from under it. It had also seen a bloody uprising during the communist era, which had been viciously repressed by the Soviets. And the city we were in, Budapest, was itself divided historically; Buda was on one side of the Danube and Pest on the other. We came rather naively into a situation of simmering conflict and division, and were immediately affected by it. We, I believe, were caught unawares, as the prevailing spirits within the nation sought to influence what we were there for, and prevent prayer for the healing of Europe from being effective. Incidentally, those simmering feelings resurfaced again in 2006 in riots, violence, racial hatred, and anti-government protests.

My own nation, England, is also affected by spiritual powers. Twenty years ago, on her first visit to England, Suzette Hattingh and I met in the home of Alan and Eileen Vincent, when they lived in Hertfordshire, just to the north of London. Gordon and Rachel Hickson were also present. Suzette told us how God had showed her in a number of places she had visited that there was a "spirit of murder" over our nation. She was particularly struck by this as she passed (not visited) the Tower of London, knowing nothing of its gruesome history. She also was surprised to "pick up the same spirit" in a cathedral as she passed the tombs of some of the knights of the Middle Ages. As we prayed about these revelations, suddenly the Holy Spirit made us aware of the abortion issue – the spirit of murder at work among the unborn – and the rocketing suicide rate, at that time the highest in Europe. As we prayed, we started to weep over our nation.

From then on, for several years, whenever the phrase "spirit of murder" or "spirit of death" in relation to our nation was mentioned, it served as a trigger in my spirit. It had the immediate effect of turning on a tap, in that I would weep uncontrollably. Sometimes this happened in embarrassing situations, once just five minutes before I was due to go on stage to lead a large prayer gathering at the Wembley Conference Centre in London. For me this was a new experience. I didn't understand what was happening and didn't know what to do about it, except to cry out to God. I recognize now that God had imparted something in my spirit that for years to come would help to shape my future ministry – but more of that later.

The significance, however, was that over our nation was a spiritual force or power of murder. I have discussed this with several other Christian leaders, and the consensus is that this spirit is linked to the "spirit of greed" – which is probably our national motivational sin. We are a materialistic society. The owning of land and possessions is part of our identity. If we are wealthy, we are said to have "made it." The apostle James writes about this:

> What causes fights and quarrels among you? Don't they come from your desires that battle within you? You want something but don't get it. You kill and covet, but you cannot have what you want. You quarrel and fight.
>
> (James 4:1–2)

How applicable are those words to British history! Greed had been institutionally at work during Britain's Empire period, when we sought the wealth of nations. Through trade, sometimes through trickery and coercion, we brought their riches to our own country. If we couldn't get what we wanted we sometimes resorted to violence and bloodshed. Sometimes we entered into treaties which were heavily weighted in our favor. When we also looked at the history within the British Isles, we saw that we English had often acted beyond necessity in slaughtering those we were seeking to subdue – in Scotland, Wales, Ireland, and even among our own people. This spirit therefore needed to be dealt with. But how, when, where, and with whom? Those questions are still being asked.

I believe that in part what some of us have been engaged in around the world, in confessing the sins of our nation committed by and through our forebears, has been a response to those questions. The only way that we can begin to counter spiritual forces at work in our society is by prayer. And the only way of overcoming the power of sin at work in our lives is through repentance and forgiveness. Whether that sin is personal to an individual or corporate within a nation, the blood of Christ is effective to provide cleansing. And if the people of God – in any nation – are implicated in committing the same acts that the nation has a reputation for, then a stronghold of evil can be established within that nation by the evil powers at work in "this dark world."

God speaks to nations as well as to individuals. As we consider the Old Testament prophets, we realize that mostly they were prophesying God's word to nations. Occasionally, of course, they had specific words to kings – both secular and God-fearing ones – but mostly their message was to nations. In the first two chapters of Amos, he is God's messenger to speak to cities, people groups, and territories (or the people within them). God's word was to Damascus (1:3), Gaza (1:6), Tyre (1:9), Edom (1:11), Ammon (1:13), Moab (2:1), and then Judah (2:4) and Israel (2:6).

In most cases, however, God's word was delivered to His people Israel. He was principally concerned that they should turn from their sin and return to Him. He was concerned that through their disobedience His name was not only dishonored among them, but also they failed to be the intended blessing to the nations (see Genesis 18:18; Ezekiel 36:22–23). So He reserves the most stinging of indictments for His own people. In them He continually saw compromise, and likens the way they behave to a wayward wife, offering her favors to all and sundry. This theme is regularly used to portray Israel consorting with pagan nations who worship false gods. What does the Lord think of us, His New Covenant people, I wonder? Have we in some ways behaved like ancient Israel?

Those who have been to India cannot but be over-whelmed by the idolatry of Hinduism and its offshoots. Temples and shrines dedicated to all kinds of gods are everywhere. On the one hand, one could say that the average Indian is very spiritually aware. The spirit world is of more concern than the physical world. Festivals and sacrifices to different gods are a recurring feature of life. And yet their spiritual awareness is at least and mostly misplaced. Idolatry is both nothing and something (1 Corinthians 8:4). Idols are lifeless and powerless. But those who worship and sacrifice to idols are making their offerings to demons (1 Corinthians 10:19–20). So, one is aware of the predominance of the demonic in much of India. Praise God for the increasing strength of the Church there, as tens of thousands of people turn to God from idols every week!

God sees the strongholds. He knows where Satan is holding people in darkness and blindness, and why. And He recognizes (as did Paul) that our eyes need to be open in order to turn from darkness to light, and from the power of Satan to God (Acts 26:18). Surely this applies both at the personal level and at the national level?

Notes

1. Pieter Bos, *The Nations Called: A Theology of the Nations and their Redemption* (Sovereign World, 2002).

CHAPTER 14

TIME TO WEEP

---------------------------≈---------------------------

THE BOOK OF LAMENTATIONS is accredited to the
authorship of Jeremiah. Because of it he is called the "weeping prophet." In it the lament that he feels over the plight
of his people is linked with the burden he carries in prayer.
Throughout his prophetic ministry he not only had to
deliver God's word of judgment to several kings, but he also
showed his anguish at what was happening to his people.

> My eyes fail from weeping,
> > I am in torment within,
> my heart is poured out on the ground
> > because my people are destroyed.

> (Lamentations 2:11)

The wound in the nation was "as deep as the sea." "Who
can heal you?" Jeremiah asks (2:13). He knows that God has
done what He planned or revealed (2:17). Then Jeremiah
calls on the "daughter of Zion" on the wall – the place
where watchmen stood guard:

> Let your tears flow like a river

> day and night;
> give yourself no relief,
>   your eyes no rest.
> Arise, cry out in the night ...
> pour out your heart like water
>   in the presence of the Lord.
>
> (Lamentations 2:18–19)

The time had come for ceaseless intercession.

Jesus also experienced weeping at times. He showed His humanity, compassion, and care when He visited the home of Mary and Martha. They told Him that His friend Lazarus, the brother of Mary and Martha, had died, and He wept (John 11:35). He also showed His anguish when He wept over Jerusalem (Luke 19:41), because the people had failed to recognize the time of God's coming to them. When He prayed in the garden, again it was in anguish. He prayed "with loud cries and tears" to the one who could save Him from death (Hebrews 5:7).

And Solomon reminded us that there is "a time to weep" (Ecclesiastes 3:4).

Tears of intercession also flowed when people prayed. Hannah wept much as she prayed about her barrenness and the ridicule of Peninnah (1 Samuel 1:10). Nehemiah wept as he heard of the condition of Jerusalem, and "mourned" continually in prayer and fasting for some days (Nehemiah 1:4). Ezra the high priest "was praying and confessing, weeping and throwing himself down before the house of God," and others were caught up in the weeping also (Ezra 10:1) – all because God's Law had been disregarded.

Questions are often asked about the experience of weeping in prayer. Is it mere emotion, or is there something more significant taking place? In the previous chapter I mentioned how the phrase "spirit of murder" began to produce in me a heart-rending, inexplicable period of weeping. For me, this was a new experience. Since then, the tears have flowed very often, particularly in situations where I am "standing in the gap" on behalf of my nation.

In Western society, men are not expected to weep. In fact in some circles it is regarded as an embarrassing sign of weakness. We are supposed to hold our emotions in check and instead display the proverbial "stiff upper lip." In recent years, however, we are getting more used to seeing images on our television screens of men weeping. Sometimes it is entirely understandable – when a loved one is lost, or when men are facing the stark horror of a bomb blast. What is becoming a more common sight is men weeping because they have just lost a football match or won a sporting championship! Emotion is part of our humanity and our natural make-up.

Tears of intercession, however, are something different, and affect both men and women. Of course our emotions are involved. But tears during intercession may be more than mere human emotion. If I am praying for a loved one or someone close to me that I care about, I may then, quite understandably, weep. My emotions are inevitably involved. But if I am praying about something with which I have no previous emotional connection then that is a different matter. And if we are seeking the face of God and wanting to be in His presence, then weeping may, for some, be a frequent experience.

The tears that Jesus shed in the Garden of Gethsemane were linked with the "great anguish" He experienced. In the garden He was "overwhelmed with sorrow to the point of death" (Mark 14:34).

> He prayed more earnestly, and his sweat was like drops of blood falling to the ground.
>
> (Luke 22:44)

The text implies that this was one of those occasions when he prayed "with loud cries and tears," but we can only conjecture about other times. His humanity and His deity conjoined to give Him an experience of intercession that was extremely hard and exhausting.

I believe that when we present ourselves to God in prayer, He is able not only to speak to us, but also to impart His burdens. If Jesus could weep on earth over Jerusalem, then heaven was involved in that. Jesus, both human and divine, combines in His prayers and intercession (they are two different things, by the way) both what He sees and knows with what His Father in heaven sees and knows. And so can we. When that happens, we become the channels through which the feelings of heaven are imparted.

We do not leave our emotions to one side in prayer. We are tripartite beings: body, mind, and spirit. So, when the Spirit of God prays through us (Romans 8:26), sighs and groans too deep for words are possible. Intercession, which has more to do with what God knows, sees, and feels, then takes place through us.

Some years ago, during the worst of the violence in Northern Ireland, I was asked to lead a prayer gathering at Spring Harvest. Having little experience of the country, and knowing less of the issues, I asked for some help from those from Northern Ireland. Among these were Leslie Spence, a Methodist minister in Lisburn and a prison chaplain to the infamous Maze prison, and Pamela Noonan, at the time head of the Board of Social Responsibility for the Presbyterian churches in the province. About 200 people gathered for this prayer time. Halfway through the meeting, a spirit of weeping was poured out on us. About half of those present, including myself, started weeping simultaneously. Later that same day, in another meeting, my wife had a similar experience during prayer for Northern Ireland (this time in the presence of the government minister responsible for Northern Ireland).

Inevitably, this led to invitations from Leslie and Pamela to visit Northern Ireland. They opened up many opportunities for me to meet church leaders across the denominational spectrum. Leslie took me into the Maze prison to meet some who were terrorists from both sides of the political/religious divide. Those I met in prison had become Christians. Previous enemies were now united, and met together to pray and study the Bible. That moved me greatly. They seemed to be freer in prison than most were in the outside world. It seemed incongruous. Here I was, an Englishman, meeting and praying with multiple murderers who were now my brothers and sisters in Christ. I wept at their stories. In fact, from the time I set foot in Northern Ireland until the time I left, I wept frequently – not just on this visit but on many subsequent ones also. Most of the time, as I was taken from place to place, I would be in prayer, and it was then that I began to discover that the tears were connected with what I was praying for.

I was taken also to some of the most notorious places in the province, including the no-man's land between the Falls Road and the Shankill Road in Belfast. I got out of the car (something my companion was too afraid to do) to walk down Coupar Way along the thirty-foot-high steel wall erected to keep the two sides apart. This was a war zone. The tops of the houses on both sides had gaping holes in their roofs, where gunfire had had its effect. This was the so-called "peace line." The Berlin Wall had come down a few years earlier, so I was angry in spirit at this symbol of division and antagonism in my own "backyard." "Does nobody care that this is here? Is nobody praying for it to come down?" I asked my friends.

Because of this concern, I was invited back to lead a prayer walk around the worst of the areas. The Lydia Fellowship in Northern Ireland and the March for Jesus committee linked up to make this happen. I was to lead it,

but had no idea what to do. But God intervened. During the
night before the prayer walk, He woke me and told me it
would become a wailing wall, and that I was to take some
eye-salve to anoint the wall in His name as a prophetic act
symbolizing His desire to open the eyes of the spiritually
blind and end the hostility.

> For he himself is our peace who has made the two one and
> has destroyed the barrier, the dividing wall of hostility.
>
> (Ephesians 2:14)

God wanted to reconcile both of them through the cross
"by which he put to death their hostility" (Ephesians 2:16).

So I did what He told me. As usual, He confirmed the
word. During our briefing period prior to the walk, one of
the ladies who lived in the area said, "The Lord woke me up
in the night and told me this would become a wailing wall,
and we were to anoint the wall"! And so it proved. When
we started to pray at the wall we started to weep, and stayed
there for some time, crying out to God in our prayers and
through our tears. The wall was anointed amidst some
powerful, faith-building prophetic words. As we started
to pray, a rainbow appeared in the sky and stayed in place
throughout our time at the wall. As we began to move
on, it became a double rainbow. We were reminded of
Genesis 9:16 about God remembering His covenant with us.
Incidentally, others who have prayed at the wall have similarly had rainbows in the sky!

Since that time I have been to Northern Ireland many
times to pray with others in many of the towns. We have
sought to dig deep into the root causes of the conflict. Reconciliation issues and events became part of what we did.
Local Christians did their research and kept me informed
ahead of our assignments. I met leaders from both sides
of the conflict: church, community, and political leaders.
Sometimes we prayed at sites of massacres or the latest

bomb outrage. Often, we discovered, a bomb went off a day or two later in the very place where we had prayed. We knew we were dealing with the supernatural powers behind so much of the hatred and bloodshed. It was almost as if Satan knew exactly what we were there for, and was seeking to demonstrate that he was in control. So we began to pray protection over the areas we visited, that no damage or injury would occur in those areas because we had been there praying. From that time on, there were no more tragedies in the areas where we prayed.

This baptism of tears often catches you unawares. In September 1999 I was leading a prayer tour for some of my American colleagues and intercessors. As mentioned in Chapter 12, Bryan Pullinger, then part of the Pray for Revival team, led a Revival Wells tour to the sites where, in the history of the British Isles, spiritual revivals had taken place. I took another group around some "heritage sites" in England, which were significant in the founding of the United States of America. Among these were visits to Cambridge and Oxford, because of their links with the universities of Harvard and Yale.

At Cambridge we were in a college, hearing of some of its history from John Martin, who had conducted Christian heritage tours of the city for many years. We were standing by the statue of William Wilberforce, the philanthropist Christian who had brought about the abolition of the slave trade through an Act of Parliament passed in 1807. Claire Sladden, one of my colleagues, was away on an errand for us. She came back just as we were ready to move on from the Wilberforce statue. Suddenly, she was overcome with deep sobs and copious tears, collapsed on the floor as she came towards us, and slid to the foot of Wilberforce, where she deposited a pool of tears. Certain people are what I call "lightning rods" for God's Spirit! They pick up what is happening in the heavenlies.

Once she was composed, we all trooped off to our next destination. I knew instinctively what the tears were about. Claire was currently doing some research in readiness for an important slave trade conference I was due to attend a couple of months later in Benin, West Africa. We had begun to realize the importance of tears from heaven in connection with what we were doing on earth. Claire confirmed that this was what the tears were about. Up until that time, I had had no spiritually strong indication about the conference, except that it was important for me to go. Now we also knew from heaven how important it was.

Her research was a key element in the Benin Conference, held in December 1999. There were twenty-five of us from Europe invited to this gathering, made up of leaders from the world of business, politics, and prayer. From Britain those who attended included Michael Fenton-Jones, leader of the International Christian Chamber of Commerce; Lord Alton, formerly a member of parliament for Liverpool, which had been a prominent slave-trade port; and myself, representing the intercessory movements. At the opening ceremony, presided over by the president of Benin, there were to be contributions from representatives of the three main groups present: the West African nations who had sold their sons and daughters into slavery; descendants of slaves from the Caribbean and the Americas (about 400 of these had made the journey); and representatives of the slave-trade nations of Europe. Michael Fenton-Jones made the European presentation, quoting some of the research Claire had provided. At the end of his speech at this opening gathering, he asked permission to engage in an act of contrition, by lying prostrate on the ground. At the same time, he asked the Europeans present to stand, to be identified with what he was doing.

As we rose to our feet, a deep wail broke out of me. I sobbed and sobbed. I couldn't stop. It was highly embarrassing. There were five African presidents there, diplomats and government ministers from many nations, plus church leaders, and a few prayer and reconciliation leaders. But the fact that we Europeans showed such depth of feeling was highly significant in the context of what was to take place in the succeeding days. The whole event was being televised and was shown across many West African nations on evening news bulletins, including the sobbing of the Europeans. Nothing could convey the reality of our shame more clearly than those tears of intercession. Claire's experience in a Cambridge college was the prelude to what happened there.

There were many more tears during the events of the following days, as we went to some of the slave-trade ports in the area, or heard from one another of the pain and upheaval created by the slave trade. In 2007 the British monarch, government, and church recognized the 200th anniversary of the Abolition of the Slave Trade Act, passed in the British Parliament in 1807, but taking three decades more to be applied in all parts of the Empire and by other nations involved in the trade.

Would to God it had been a celebration of 200 years without slavery! Even today, unfortunately, the slave trade is still engaged in by some Arab traders, and by those who coerce children into being sex-slaves, and women into prostitution, or who control cheap labor in the sweat shops of the developing world.

We, the British, followed the Abolition of the Slave Trade by introducing a scheme of indentured labor by which cheap labor was recruited from India as a substitute for slavery. In the years following the passing of this Act, we thus created a new diaspora of Indians – in the Caribbean, parts of South America, Uganda, Kenya, Malaysia, Singapore, and Fiji. This was meant to replace slavery, but it was slavery by another name. These cheap labor schemes still persist in many forms throughout the world, with those recruited often living in appalling conditions and getting a pittance for their labors. Maybe a lot more tears will have to be shed by those who will pray for all those who are manipulated into modern forms of slavery.

It's a time to weep with the tears of heaven. If Jesus was anguished over the sin of the world 2,000 years ago, what must He feel now? There is so much that could cause Him to weep. What a disappointment we as the Church on earth must be to Him! We still haven't filled the earth with His glory. There are still thousands of tribes not reached with the gospel, and with no indigenous church. Nations are still fighting one another over ancient hatreds. The innocent blood of millions of people continues to be shed. Despite huge scientific advances, poverty and pandemic diseases continue to enslave millions.

Where are those who will "stand in the gap" over these and many other issues? Where are those who will carry as a prayer burden the plight of those without hope and without God?

> He who goes out weeping,
>   carrying seed to sow,
> will return with songs of joy,
>   carrying sheaves with him.

(Psalm 126:6)

CHAPTER 15

CONFESSING AND REPENTING

IN JAMES CHAPTER 5, WE READ ABOUT PRAYER offered in faith. It has to do with the healing of the sick, anointing with oil and the calling of elders. Mostly, we apply that to individual healing, and rightly so. Forgiveness of sins of the sick person is linked to the prayer offered in faith.

> Therefore confess your sins to each other and pray for each other so that you may be healed. The prayer of a righteous man is powerful and effective.
>
> (James 5:16)

For prayer and intercession to be effective, it needs to be sin-free. If we cherish sin in our hearts, the Lord will not hear us (see Psalm 66:18). Not that He can't hear, but He won't. Sin is in the way.

Without confessing and repenting of that sin, my relationship with God, and therefore the effectiveness of my prayer, is hindered. God will, however, hear the prayers of righteous men and women. So confession and repentance is the key to effective prayer. King David in his prayer of confession in Psalm 51 had realized this. He knew that his broken spirit and contrite heart were necessary to bring the cleansing he needed.

What is true of us individually is also true of us corporately or representationally. Ongoing sickness and unanswered prayer are linked to unconfessed sin and unrighteous intercessors! When individuals begin to take responsibility before God for the sin of their group, tribe or denomination, then the door is open for some corporate healing to take place. We see this depicted often through the prayer of individuals, acting as intercessors for their people (as in Daniel 9; Nehemiah 1; Ezra 9 and 10).

As we also saw in Chapter 7, the message of God to the seven churches of Asia Minor was, "Repent!" Sin had crept in. Individual sin had become church sin. Although there was responsibility on the part of the individuals concerned, the message was corporate to the churches: repent.

There is a difference between confession and repenting. By *confessing* something, I merely acknowledge with my mouth that there is a problem, that sin has taken place. No change of heart or of practice is intended or signified by the use of the word "confess." But we know that without *repentance* and a change of attitude, there can be no forgiveness and cleansing. God is always looking for changed hearts and attitudes. He wants us to be cleansed. Through repentance or by "repenting," I am saying that I want to be changed, to see change, and to be an instrument for changed behavior.

In "confession" there is not the same strength of meaning. The Greek word *metanoia*, which is consistently translated as "repentance" or "repent," involves both a change of mind about sin, and a change of heart-attitude towards sin. The idea of reformation (of character) and of reversal of another's decision is also implied in the use of the word. So it is possible to repent for another's sin.

God is speaking to His Church the world over about the need for repentance of corporate sin – past and present, ancient and modern. He wants His bride to be "without spot or blemish." So, in nation after nation, the corporate sin of the Church, and of the nation of which it is part, is being revealed and identified by the Holy Spirit. The Church is being called to a time of purification.

This is extremely important, particularly in those nations where church and state have become closely intertwined. In some nations there is a so-called state church – that is, a church that is recognized as the church of the state. This is particularly so in Europe. Whether we look at Orthodox East, Catholic West, or Protestant North, nearly all European nations have known a very strong "church–state" connection over hundreds of years of history. Also in other countries there may be a strong relationship which affects everything the Church or the state does. For instance, there has always been a strong connection between the president of the United States and the churches of the nation. The "religious right," as it is called, makes sure its voice is heard in matters of the state, and successive presidents have been at pains to show how their religious beliefs inform their political policies. Nothing wrong with that, of course, but the implications are, therefore, that sins of the state and those of the Church are sometimes indistinguishable.

Of course, this state connection also exists strongly within other religious systems. In nearly every nation where Islam is strong, it portrays the whole nation as being Islamic (even though in practice many ethnic and tribal groups may not have embraced Islam). Also, too, in Buddhist nations there is a deliberate attempt to link Buddhist teaching and practice with the way in which those nations are led politically. Nepal is the world's only Hindu state, so the affairs of state there are informed by and connected with the practice of Hinduism. However, let's confine our consideration to those nations that regard themselves as "Christian," and to what happens when a few individuals take Scripture seriously enough to stand before God on behalf of their own sins and the sin of their nation or group, even when they have limited theological understanding.

One of the repercussions from the break-up of the communist bloc has been the re-emergence of latent nationalism. States which had previously been invaded and then controlled by the Russians, as part of the Soviet Union, have discovered once again their national identity.

This was radically shown in the former Yugoslavia, itself a federation of previously independent states, but operating with close affinity to communist, Soviet-led Eastern Europe. Early in the 1990s the so-called Bosnian War erupted. This was not a new conflict; it was more a repeat of history. The Balkans had seen conflict for centuries, each war seeking to be a settling of old scores. We refer to it as part of the "fault line" of Europe, which has a strong religious dimension to it. Going back centuries, this region had experienced religious conflicts between the East (predominantly Orthodox) and the West (predominantly Catholic). Since the spread of the Ottoman Empire, a third influence – that of Islam – intruded into the region, notably into Albania, Kosovo, and Bosnia.

The Bosnian War was a wider conflagration in which Slovenia, Montenegro, Macedonia (to a lesser extent), Croatia, Bosnia, and Serbia were involved. All of these states were part of the former Republic of Yugoslavia and sought to secede after the fall of communism. The Serbs saw it as an opportunity for the redefining of what they regard as Greater Serbia. The Serbs fought both the Croats and the Bosnians, the Croats fought both the Serbs and the Bosnians, and the Bosnians fought back. Each nation had the prevalent religious system giving its blessing. Into the mix came the United Nations, seeking to "keep the peace" with placements of soldiers throughout the region; these, however, were not supposed to open fire except in self-defense.

As this was a European conflict, we sought to raise prayer for what was going on. Through the Evangelical

Alliance we developed a number of initiatives, including prayer days, prayer weeks, and social action initiatives. Partnerships were developed between churches and ministries to bring aid across the borders into all of the countries affected. Trevor Gregory, my assistant at the Evangelical Alliance at the time, had a five-year old son, called Luke. Luke prayed every meal-time for the children of Bosnia. Trevor came up with the idea of running a "Luke Appeal" - to make up shoeboxes of gifts from children in schools and Sunday schools across the country. Thousands of children, and hundreds of schools and Sunday schools, participated in this. At the same time, Paul Brooks, formerly of Youth for Christ, developed a project called Novi Most, based on the symbol of the old bridge uniting East and West Mostar in Bosnia, which had been an early casualty of the war. (*Novi Most* translates as "New Bridge.")

In the summer of 1994 I made my first visit to the region with a couple of friends, to conduct a prayer school among young people at a camp on the Adriatic coast. During that visit, I met several of the significant Christian leaders in the emerging state of Croatia. We wanted to go into the war zone to pray but were advised against it, because of the dangers.

Then, early in 1995, God said to me one day, "I want you to go to Bosnia with a prayer team." I asked Him when, and He seemed to indicate a week in August that year. I tried to raise a prayer team with some of my friends, but surprisingly no one was free or burdened to be part of it! But I kept the dates open. Three days before the time came for me to go, I still had no plans. Then I received a fax from John Robb, prayer coordinator for World Vision. I had met John for the first time in Korea in 1993, but we had never previously worked together. In his fax he said, "I am leading a prayer team to Bosnia, and God has told me that I have to invite you." The prayer journey was due to start the exact date I had already marked off in my diary, but was due to last ten days. I cleared my diary for the rest of the ten days, checked the airline, and booked a cheap last-minute flight to Split. I also took the precaution of making a will – just in case!

We all met in Mostar, a terribly bombed city in Bosnia. Karmelo Kresonja, a church leader there, facilitated our visit. The guest house we stayed in had sustained some bomb damage. We met up with Nikola and Sandra Skrin-jaric, a remarkable couple who had planted several churches during the war, despite the dangers. Our prayer journey took us from Mostar to Tuzla – a journey that lasted nine hours and entailed negotiating perilous mountain roads and tracks, skirting frontline positions of the Serb forces. We were stopped at twenty-five checkpoints – some United Nations, others manned by Croat or Bosnian forces – as we wove in and out of the various pockets of territory. It really was a prayer journey!

We ministered in three of the newly planted churches during our time there: two in Mostar and one in Tuzla. What was remarkable was that in each of these churches were new Christians, most having been believers for less than two years. In each place, we talked about reconciliation as the means in God's hand to bring about an end to hostilities. In each place these new Christians, from Serb, Croat, and Bosnian Muslim backgrounds, were in the meetings. All of them had suffered, through loss of family members, personal injury, and loss of their homes or businesses. So the pain – and blame – was acute. But God so touched them that, in each meeting, different individuals stood up to confess their antagonism and hatred of the other side, and of the sins of their own side. They repented of their own part in the hostilities, and asked for forgiveness. It really was very moving. Tears flowed a lot. Because they were in Christ, they were now able to reconcile with their previous enemies. We as a team also repented of the sins of the Western nations that had contributed to the pain and loss they were suffering. Theological understanding was not the issue here. Corporate pain, and the climate of fear and antagonism, needed healing, and the ongoing conflict needed to be brought to an end. These ordinary, new Christians were able to embrace the need for repentance and reconciliation between one another and between their various groups.

We met with leaders of the Orthodox and Catholic churches in Tuzla. We sought to pray with everyone we met and at some of the sites of massacres. We were taken by UNHCR aid workers to visit Tuzla airport where thousands of refugees – victims of the Srebrenica massacre – had been placed in tents. Mostly they were women and children; hardly a man was to be seen. It was an appalling sight. I held a two-week-old baby in my arms. She had been born on the airport tarmac. One of our team took off his shoes and gave them to an old woman whose shoes were unwearable. We felt so helpless in the face of so much human need.

When the time came for us to return to Mostar, and then out of Bosnia into Croatia, we were not stopped once at any checkpoint. "Something has happened. Something has changed," we commented to each other. And then beyond Mostar, we passed a huge convoy of United Nations peacekeeping forces and equipment on its way into the war zone. Whilst we were on the ground praying, and getting many prophetic words about a cessation of hostilities, and that the last bomb had fallen, a peace agreement was being signed. The war had ended. God had orchestrated us going at that precise time in order for us to deal in prayer with the spiritual factors behind the conflict. The full account of this remarkable story is written up in *The Peace-making Power of Prayer* by John Robb and James Hill.[1]

This story illustrates the importance of not only hearing God's voice but also obeying it. It also shows how significant confession and repentance is in bringing about the spiritual conditions for healing and cleansing. There have been many situations since, where the power of this has been amply demonstrated, not only in personal healing of body, mind, and spirit, but also in the healing of nations. God is truly awesome in how He works and the way in which He includes us.

A couple of years ago, I was in Jerusalem for thirty-six hours as part of a five-day visit to Israel. As we were staying near the site of the Garden Tomb, I said to my colleague, who wished to rest, that I would walk to it. On arrival, I found that my long-term friends, Victor Jack (chairman of the Garden Tomb Association) and his wife Meg, were also there. So Victor offered to show me around. As I walked into the garden, the Holy Spirit said to me, "Where were you three weeks ago?"

The question took me by surprise. What had I been doing? Then I remembered: I had been in the United States. I looked at my watch, did a time-zone check, and suddenly realized that at this precise time three weeks before, I had been walking into a cinema near Boston with my son Philip to see the film *The Passion of Christ.* Now here I was, walking into the very arena where the scenes depicted in the film actually took place. It was an awesome moment! As I reached the garden tomb, like many before me, no doubt, I knelt down on the stone pavement and began to weep. Here Jesus' body had lain. Nearby was the hill on which He had been crucified and where He prayed, "Father, forgive them, for they do not know what they are doing."

Suddenly it hit me. Here, in Jerusalem, was where He prayed that prayer. Here in this city above all cities is where forgiveness is hard to find. And here, in this city, is where that prayer is still to be answered. Palestinians and Israelis are fighting one another. Muslims and Jews are fighting one another. Even Christians are fighting one another with words. You can be a Palestinian Christian, an Arab Christian, a Messianic believer, an Orthodox Christian, a Western Protestant Christian, and so on, and not find a place of unity with your fellow believers. It is a city of such division and complex politics that it seems almost impossible for that prayer to be answered. Yet, here, Jesus prayed that prayer. He knows that His prayers will always be answered, even if, for the time being, the enemy of God and of us is frustrating God's will.

In my naivety, I still believe that through repenting of our sins, both personally and corporately, it is possible for things to change – even in Jerusalem. But those so separated by ancient hostilities will only find a way of peace through mutual repentance and forgiveness. They all need to be forgiven. But not to admit their guilt will effectively bar the way to change.

When Jesus prayed the "Forgive them" prayer, it was for those who were doing Him harm, those who were killing Him. It was a prayer for His murderers. Who were the guilty ones? The Roman soldiers? The Jewish leaders? The crowds who surrounded Him? The one who betrayed Him? The disciples who denied Him and then fled from Him? Or those who cried, "Crucify him"?

What is true of the Jerusalem of Jesus' time is true today in the multitude of situations in every nation, where corporate sin remains unconfessed and therefore unforgiven, where ancient hatreds continue to simmer in unholy anger, and where resentment and revenge are allowed to fester. Only when those who understand the miracle and grace of forgiveness begin to live it out through repentance, can they begin to make a difference.

As Jesus looks at the Jerusalem of today, and at similar troubled, divided cities across this planet, He sees that nobody is righteous. Guilt is shared by all. And therefore all need to repent, forgive and be forgiven, and so be reconciled – both to God and to one another.

Notes

1. John Robb and James Hill, *The Peace-making Power of Prayer* (Broadman and Holman, 2000).

CHAPTER 16

RECONCILIATION AND
PREPARING THE WAY

———————— ≈ ————————

THE SPIRIT OF GOD HAS BEEN SPEAKING to Christian leaders around the world about the need to heal the wounds of history and to be the instruments to bring about reconciliation. Sometimes that reconciliation is necessary between churches of different denominations, sometimes we need to stand in the gap on behalf of our nation or group, and sometimes we become the catalyst to encourage reconciliation between others.

Particularly, however, God has been speaking about the corporate more than about the individual. The need for individuals to be reconciled with those from whom they have become separated through sin and division is, of course, ongoing. But God also wants to deal with corporate entities.

Reconciliation horizontally is not an end in itself; it is the means to a greater end. Take, for example, a church that has split because of dispute and has divided into two or more groups, spawning separate places of worship. In the past, those splits have sometimes been very public, in that the alternative place of worship has been established in the same street, almost as near to the "mother church" as possible. The repercussions of such acrimonious rivalry calls into question the public credibility of those church groups, even for decades and centuries afterwards. So, if and when there is reconciliation between the separated groups, not only is there healing between them, but also the repercussions in the wider community begin to be felt. No longer is disunity a bar to the spread of the gospel. On the contrary, the new-found unity becomes a springboard for greater effectiveness.

God says,

> "Build up, build up, prepare the road!
>   Remove the obstacles out of the way of my people."
> For this is what the high and lofty One says –
>   he who lives for ever, whose name is holy:
> "I live in a high and holy place,
>   but also with him who is contrite and lowly in spirit."
>
> (Isaiah 57:14–15)

Then God goes on to talk about His rage at our greed, our willful ways and our wickedness, and His desire to heal us. What is the prerequisite? We need to humble ourselves and confess our sin, past and present. He has a plan for us Christians, and for His bride, the Church, to be a blessing to the nations – and this is it.

> Pass through, pass through the gates!
>   Prepare the way for the people.
> Build up, build up the highway!
>   Remove the stones.
> Raise a banner for the nations.
>
> (Isaiah 62:10)

What are the stones? What are the obstacles to blessing? What causes the highway, the road, to be unfit for purpose? Is it not unconfessed sin? What do we have to do to prepare the way for God to work? A holy God cannot ignore our sin and pretend that it didn't happen or that it doesn't matter any more. It needs to be moved out of the way in our lives – again, both at the individual as well as the corporate level. And these aren't merely the sins of the moment – of this day or this week, or even this year. They are also the sins of history. How can the corporate sins of our forebears be cleansed if there hasn't been any confession or repentance? Do we have to bear the reproach of heaven because our forebears have passed on? Or can we today do something about it? If the historic blockages had already been removed, then surely we would be enjoying great blessing. But our historic sin is huge!

Roger Mitchell and I have written about this in our book, *Sins of the Fathers*. [1] Many nations throughout the world have something against Britain. Our historic sins against them have continued to cause antagonism, resentment, opposition and hatred, leading to many recriminations. How can this cycle be broken? Is it important for it to be broken? And who is qualified to do something about it?

The message in that book has found echoes in many other nations, with a history of wounding or being wounded. Over the last sixty years, German Christians have had to live with the legacy and shame of the Nazi era. It has become a national offense to succeeding generations. To their credit, there have been many occasions when German Christians (even those without a Second World War history) have apologized to the nations against whom the Fuhrer, Adolf Hitler, and his followers sinned so grossly. We are talking about the killing of millions of Europeans, from every nation of Europe. We are talking about the Holocaust and the slaughter of millions of Jews in gas ovens. We are talking about the invasion and captivity of many nations. Huge wartime cemeteries exist, particularly in the killing fields of France and Belgium. Not every German was involved, of course, but the corporate guilt of that era does affect the entire nation.

The seeds of Nazism still, alas, remain in some. But the shame and the guilt felt by many Christians have been expressed again and again. Some years ago, long-distance prayer walks took place from Berlin, the capital, to every nation that Germany had invaded during the 1939–45 War. Young Germans, and their parents and grandparents, took part in these walks. Christians from those nations invaded by Germany also joined in. These became walks of reconciliation and unity. The first walk from London to Berlin served to stimulate the rest, and the initiators, John and Yvonne Pressdee, moved to Germany to partner with the Germans and help them with the process.

On the Berlin to Moscow expedition, we arrived at the border with Poland. East and West Germany had already been reunited following the breaking down of the Berlin Wall in 1989, but Poland was still fiercely guarding its borders. Over 100 of us on the walk had to wait at Frankfurt-am-Oder for permission to cross over. Once across, we were met by Polish Christian leaders. A gathering between West and East had been arranged at an open-air plaza near the River Oder.

During the Second World War, millions of Poles had been incarcerated in concentration camps or conscripted into the German army. Many thousands had also fled as refugees to other European nations. The Polish national identity was taken away; the country became part of Germany. Some of the worst atrocities against Jews were committed in Poland. So the offense against the Poles was huge. We were told that, because of this history, Poles hated the Germans. One can understand why!

The German Christians had brought with them a flag for each of the states of Germany. Young Germans lined up on this plaza in front of the Poles and, as the prepared words of repentance and reconciliation were read out, we all knelt on the ground. The flags of Germany, once used as a sign of their people's superiority and paraded arrogantly, were now lowered to the ground as a sign of their contrition. There were many tears shed – by Poles, Germans, and by those of us from other nations. Strangely, as we were weeping, giant raindrops fell from the sky on us all. It was almost as if God's tears were cascading down with ours. The whole scene was very moving.

This "ceremony" was captured by the television cameras that had turned up to witness the ceremony. Later, reports appeared on evening television news in both Poland and Germany. What a difference this made! When we continued the prayer walking the next day, we saw the effects. The Germans were expecting to receive a hostile reception because of the nationally felt antagonism towards them. But the atmosphere had changed. Instead, crowds of people turned out to welcome the walkers as we passed through villages and towns. We came to one township where there were many large apartment blocks, built around a makeshift park that doubled as a football pitch. Local Christians, Catholic and Protestant, had erected a stage, and invited us to take over. Every balcony around the apartment blocks was crowded with people, and there were many hundreds of people on the football pitch. Reconciliation had opened the way for us to share more and to bring God's Word to many thousands of open hearts. I doubt any of this would have happened without the Germans first of all repenting as they stepped onto Polish soil.

Most can relate to this kind of process, since the Second World War is within the living memory of many of the older generation. But those who take part in these events are usually much younger, without personal history or blame accruing to them. Nevertheless, they are the undoubted inheritors of what took place in the 1939–45 War and they live with the consequences. Take that on a century or two, and will it be any different? By then, attitudes will have been passed on to the succeeding generations. Feelings of antagonism will remain and, without reconciliation, will emerge in different forms in the unfolding story of nations, as has happened in many other situations around the globe.

There can be few events in history that reflect this more than the Crusades of the eleventh and twelfth centuries. These were religious crusades, mounted in Europe, with the intention of keeping open pilgrimage routes to the Holy Land. Unfortunately, the religious intentions became diluted. Into the mix came all the antagonisms felt against people of other faiths, or other parts of the Christian world. So these Crusaders, made up of many types of people, some with little or no faith, but led by knights sporting a red cross emblazoned across their tunics, went into battle against all and sundry. On the way to the Holy Land (not once but many times over nearly a century), they slaughtered Jews, Muslims, people of Orthodox faith, and some groups who had sought to express an early form of Protestantism (without calling it that). Some of these crusades started in France, some in Germany, and some in England. Kings and priests were involved. It was said that when they arrived in Jerusalem the streets ran with the blood of those slaughtered!

The fact that the Crusades were apparently religiously inspired, with religious objectives, made the bloodshed abhorrent to God and to people of many backgrounds. It has become an historic blockage to official dealings of Christian leaders with those of Islamic and Jewish faiths, and between individual Christians, Muslims, and Jews. Even today, Muslim nations refer to the "crusading West." When they see what they understand as "Christian nations" going to war, they see us repeating the sins of history, thus creating anger and ongoing resentment. This not only hinders relationships and understanding between nations, it also prevents the gospel having effect. Those nations where Christians experience most persecution are, not surprisingly, Muslim nations. As Muslims see it, it is a sin – even a betrayal – to convert to Christianity, whereas we know that what occurs is a conversion to a Person, Jesus Christ, not to a historic, flawed, unbiblical system. Those who do convert prefer to be known, therefore, as "followers of Jesus", not as "Christians."

So between 1996 and 1999 a series of "reconciliation" prayer walks was mounted along the routes taken by the Crusaders up to 900 years previously. This was simply called The Reconciliation Walk, although there were many walks in many nations. Lynn Green and John Pressdee were the principal leaders. They are two others that in eternity will have stories to tell of how God led them into these expeditions, what transpired, and what have been the ongoing consequences. Even for me to tell some of the story now would be premature, and might even put people at risk. What I can say is that this walk was noticed and commented on by the media in many nations, including Britain, Turkey, and Israel. It also produced countless stories of changed attitudes towards Christians, and openness to the Christ that they serve. The non-Christian world understands the need for repentance and reconciliation far more readily, it seems, than do some Christian leaders.

Those involved in national and international reconciliation ministry make no claims that their endeavors have been entirely successful. We are all still on a journey. Some wounds are so deep that it may take a generation for lasting change to be apparent. And when something prompted by the Spirit of God is being done, from God's perspective that may be but the first step. Jesus' death on the cross was not immediately seen as "successful," but for all of time it stands as a monument to God's grace and power. In retrospect, we see how the spiritual battle was being won, and how forgiveness was being made available. Paul's words to the church at Colosse sums it up:

> He forgave us all our sins, having canceled the written code, with its regulations, that was against us and that stood opposed to us; he took it away, nailing it to the cross. And having disarmed the powers and authorities, he made a public spectacle of them, triumphing over them by the cross.
>
> (Colossians 2:13–15)

That was a retrospective comment on Paul's part. The outworking of it is still occurring 2,000 years later.

When God put on our hearts the need for reconciliation between England and Australia, we began a journey for which we had no blueprint or roadmap. We had to learn as we journeyed, listen to the Holy Spirit, and do what He said. The dawning of the need to do something started at a conference in Korea in 1993. A breakfast conversation at the GCOWE Conference in 1995 led to an opportunity to put down a public marker. A year later, I visited Australia and from the airport went to see the new leader of the Australian prayer movement, Brian Pickering, to share our concern to come and say "Sorry" for the past. Within a year, Roger Mitchell made a short reconnaissance trip, and had some amazing divine appointments.

Then in 1998 we led a team of up to thirty intercessors over a seven-week period to every state of Australia to say "Sorry" three or four times a day for the sins of our 200-year history with Australia. We were just doing what God had laid on our hearts to do, without any idea as to the outcome. A year later, thirty-five Australians, from both white and aboriginal background, came to England to say "We forgive you" in multiple locations. Now, looking back, we can say that Australia has changed. The rebellious "teenage nation" (to quote Brian Pickering) has come of age and is taking its place in the family of nations. Is everything perfect? No. Have all the wounds been healed? No. Is there still more to do? Most certainly. But progress has been, and still is being, made. You can read the fuller story in *Fountains of Tears*,[2] available from me at the address at the end of the book.

So where do we start in this journey? Surely it must be among ourselves. We have found that usually (but not always) God starts by alerting those with an intercessory prayer burden about certain issues requiring healing. And usually these are on both sides of whatever the divide may be. Those with that intercessory connection then become God's instruments for the first stage of engagement: repentance between those who pray, taking responsibility for whatever the sins are, on behalf of whatever the corporate entity is. Later, church leadership and even political leadership become involved. But at first, it seems, God alerts those with a priestly calling about what He sees, and about the timing. There is a time for all these things. I don't know why we are at this time in a season of repentance and reconciliation. But we are, and we need to do what God wants, when He wants.

I would never have dreamed of embarking on a ministry of reconciliation, had not the Spirit of God brought home to me the anguish that heaven feels over unrepented sin. For the past fifteen years I have carried the "pain" of being English. Recently I have listened in anguish as Irishmen in a pub recounted to one another the wrongs of the English, historically as well as recently. I cringed as Afrikaans businessmen, without any prompting, told of their antagonism because their grandfathers were killed by the English. I watched a Kenyan leader speak on television of the legacy of the British in his country. I heard the heart-cry

of a Sudanese Christian leader as he said, with tears, that his
country was in a mess, and the reason was because of the
legacy of the English. The repercussions are with us today.
We cannot ignore them.

Some years ago, during a prayer time with others, God
showed me a battlefield. Scattered around it were burned-
out equipment and dead bodies – people with broken limbs
and blackened faces, their clothes hanging off their bodies
like rags. It was a sight of utter devastation. I asked God
what it was. "This is my Church," He said. "This is how I
see things. The wounds you have received, however, are self-
inflicted. You have done all this to one another."

If that is true, how can we be healed? Surely, this can
only occur as we bind up one another's wounds and, instead
of inflicting more pain and injury, begin to love and care for
one another. When we start to acknowledge the wounds
we have committed against one another and repent of the
attitudes behind them – anger, resentment, hatred, criticism, slander, greed, fear – then God will begin to do a new
thing among us, and bring healing through us. That process will begin to *prepare the way* for His bride to be viewed
differently, so that she can become the channel of love
and beauty.

God intends us to be the instruments of reconciliation. But if there are areas in us personally or corporately
that are unreconciled, and if there are others with whom
there is ongoing antagonism, then we will fail to be those
instruments. And the world around us will suffer. Reconciliation, from God's viewpoint, is with Himself, then with
one another. But from the perspective of non-believers
it is the other way around. When they see us being reconciled with one another, the door is more open for
them to be reconciled through Christ with God (see 2
Corinthians 5:16–21). Reconciliation is neither a theory,
nor a theological concept only. It is a practical way of

bringing us into relationship with God and with one another. It has to work!

Notes

1. Brian Mills and Roger Mitchell, *Sins of the Fathers: How National Repentance Removes Obstacles for Revival* (Sovereign World, 1999).

2. Brian Mills, *Fountains of Tears: Changing Nations through the Power of Repentance and Forgiveness* (Sovereign World, 2004).

CHAPTER 17

PARTNERSHIPS IN PRAYER

———————— ≈ ————————

I AM NOT A GOOD PRAY-ER. Although I love praying and being in the presence of God, I am not a good prayer. Like many others, I find that my mind tends to wander, and the discipline of prolonged prayer on my own is often a struggle. Notwithstanding, I want to persevere, because I know the joy of prayer where the presence of God is real and where I can draw closer to Him. From such communion with our Father, I get to know Him better and know when He is speaking. It is then that answers flow.

Like many others also, I have found that praying with one or two others is quite different. The dynamics of being with someone else who wants the same as you are always mutually strengthening. Most of the really fulfilling times of prayer, when breakthrough is being achieved, have been in the company of others. This book is ample testimony to that. Nearly everything that God told me to do was to be worked out with others. God views unity as vital. He also knows we need to be strengthened by partnerships in prayer. Jesus said:

Where two or three come together in my name, there am I
with them.

(Matthew 18:20)

Throughout the Bible there are some wonderful partnerships in prayer. Moses, Aaron, and Hur were linked together
in prayer (both physically and spiritually) on the hilltop,
whilst Joshua was fighting the battle against the Amalekites
in the valley below (Exodus 17:8–16). That partnership was
crucial in achieving victory.

For hands were lifted up to the throne of the Lord.

(Exodus 17:16)

One of the classic prayer partnerships of the Bible is that
of Moses and Joshua. The two of them went together up
Mount Sinai to meet with God, when Moses received the
Ten Commandments (Exodus 24:13). The two of them
also entered the Tent of Meeting to meet with the Lord,
when the pillar of cloud and the glory of God came down
(Exodus 33:7–11).

The relationship between David and his son, Solomon,
is interesting. They shared a common sense of destiny, a
burden to build a temple in Jerusalem as a permanent place
where the presence of God could be experienced. They also
shared a personal relationship with God, of which Psalms
and Proverbs are ample testimony. David wanted to bring
the ark of God back to Jerusalem. Solomon dedicated the
temple to the Lord in prayer and had the ark placed in it.
In both cases, God demonstrated His powerful presence.
David enjoyed another strong partnership, with Jonathan,
the son of King Saul. This partnership survived even the bit-
ter opposition shown by Saul towards David.

Daniel and his three friends, Hananiah, Mishael, and
Azariah (their original names), shared some amazing
experiences of prayer. It was their all-night prayer that led

to Daniel receiving revelation about Nebuchadnezzar's dream (Daniel 2). It was their resolute faith and willingness to stand together and not compromise their beliefs, which resulted in them being saved from the fiery furnace (Daniel 3).

And then Jesus, on two occasions when He needed the companionship of others in prayer, took with Him the same three disciples – Peter, James, and John – onto the Mount of Transfiguration and into the Garden of Gethsemane. Unfortunately, in both cases the three fell asleep!

Yet, despite that apparent failure, it was the importance of prayer that carried them and the other disciples through after the resurrection and ascension of Jesus, as they sought to live out His principles. In Acts 1:14, after Jesus had been taken from them into the sky, "they all joined together constantly in prayer." They were in prayer when the Holy Spirit was poured out among them (Acts 2:1–4). Peter and John resorted to prayer with others after the Sanhedrin released them and placed restrictions on them (Acts 4:23–31). They emphasized the priority of prayer when problems developed (Acts 6:4). Peter and John went to Samaria to pray for the new believers to receive the Holy Spirit (Acts 8:14–17). And it was the Church at prayer that led to angelic intervention and the supernatural release of Peter from prison (Acts 12:1–10). The new partnership of Paul and Barnabas developed out of the praying church at Antioch (Acts 13:1–3). God wants us in partnerships of prayer.

Partnerships with others

Most of the church prayer meetings I used to attend were rather mundane affairs. Prayer was a duty more than a delight. We prayed for our members, our activities, and our missionaries. That was mostly it. Nothing wrong with that, but a spark was missing. When God gave me the idea of prayer triplets (see Chapter 3), I could not have foreseen how crucial were to be the relationships that developed in these groups. I have heard many say, "I may miss some of the church activities, but one thing I never want to miss is the prayer triplet group." A close partnership in prayer developed in such groups. They prayed for others, yes, but they also prayed for themselves. Some of those groups lasted many years and were something of a "lifesaver" for those in lonely and difficult situations.

Women involved in Lydia prayer groups feel the same. The Lydia Fellowship is huge and now international. But at its heart it is a fellowship of small groups of praying women who pray what God gives them for their nation and the nations. The key element in these partnerships is prayer for and with each other.

In the prayer group that my wife, Ruth, and I were part of in Wokingham, England, it was also like that. Our partnership with a group of about fifteen people was so important to us all, that more than twenty years later we still meet together and pray for each other and our families.

Partnerships for others

When Peter Wagner wrote his book *Prayer Shield*,[1] he was articulating what many had found to be true: the strength of commitment in prayer in support of others. Many missionaries know this from years of experience in a country other than their own. There are some fantastic stories of how God has answered prayer by such shields at times of danger and challenge. Many people in so-called frontline ministry have cultivated and relied on such prayer shields. (A "prayer shield" consists of a number of dedicated prayer partners who are committed to be in prayer daily for a particular person or persons in ministry, and to be available to the Holy Spirit's prompting.)

Years ago, I felt prompted by God to invite certain individuals who had shown interest in us and in what we were doing to cover us daily in prayer. I regularly informed them of upcoming challenges and opportunities, and occasionally visited them to fill in more of the detail. Sometimes an "SOS" would be sent via home to alert them to urgent needs. This group was a vital lifeline, particularly when I was in situations of danger.

Once, I was driving in my hometown, when suddenly my mind was filled with swear words, and I was filled with thoughts of driving at breakneck speed in a restricted area. I knew I was under demonic attack and in a spiritual battle. I cried out to God, "Lord, please get someone praying!" As soon as I could, I parked in a quiet place near the River Thames, and prayed.

Later that day, I was having a phone conversation with a vicar friend in Lancashire. His wife came on the other end of the line. "Brian," she said, "what on earth was happening this morning at [such-and-such a time]? I had to stop what I was doing and call out to God for you." In a broken voice, I thanked her and told her what was happening at the precise time that God had alerted her.

A few months after the conclusion of the evangelistic phase of Mission England, I met someone at a conference, whom I knew a little. He said to me, "I'm glad you've finished with Mission England. I can now get a good night's sleep."

"What do you mean?" I asked.

He replied, "For months, God has been waking me in the middle of the night, every night, around 3 a.m. to pray for you."

I wept and thanked him. I then told him how major crises had occurred in the families of each of my colleagues in the Mission England team. Two were involved in serious accidents, another had attacks on his family, and others had serious health issues. I was the only one, it seemed, who survived unscathed. It was due, I am sure, to the prayers of unknown (and known) prayer partners.

Partnerships for ministry

"Can I partner with you?" asked Jeff Marks of me as we traveled together in a car to a reconciliation event in Scotland. Jeff was a North American prayer leader, leading New England Concerts of Prayer. He and I had known each other for many years, and we both believed that God wanted to do something special through links between New England and (old) England, because of our common heritage. We had already participated in prayer events and tours together on both sides of the Atlantic. We were beginning to embark on a journey of reconciliation over some of the issues that contributed to the plight of Native Americans in his country, and over the unhealed separation of white Americans and English epitomized by the American War of Independence.

Initially, I was unsure of this idea of partnership, although I already had some connections within England, which had been developed through a ministry called Interprayer. Then God said, "You take on what I give you to do and the people I send to you, and I will provide the resources you need." So eventually I said "Yes" to Jeff, without knowing what I was saying "Yes" to or letting myself in for. Jeff became our first international partner.

About the same time, I was asked to meet up with John Mulinde (from Uganda), who was making his first visit to England. As I was out of the country, my ministry partner, David Sladden, made the connection. On my return he phoned me, saying I needed to put myself out to try and meet with John. We managed to find an hour together just before he was to leave to return to Uganda. That was the start of a friendship and a linking in ministry that has persisted. David in particular opened many doors for ministry for John in the United Kingdom and in other parts of Europe, and often traveled with him. Since then, John and I have ministered together in several other nations, including our own.

Again around the same time, Linda Holt, at that time heading up prayer for the Methodist Headway organization, approached me about a closer link. I thought she would be a good prayer partner, but God said it was to be more than that: "She needs to be in a working partnership with you." With her heart also to help release children and young people in prayer, she brought a different dimension. So we invited her to be linked with us more formally. We began discussing the way we should operate as a male and female partnership, without the risk of sexual overtones intruding or unwarranted suspicions complicating what we were trying to achieve. So we intentionally began to include our spouses in the invitation to be with us when we met together. That has continued to this day, whether or not our spouses individually have a prayer ministry. We reckon that if God has joined us together in marriage we are also inevitably partnering in some way in ministry.

And so the partnership has continued to grow. Sometimes individual leaders approach one or more of us to ask if they can be included in the partnership. At other times we feel that God is leading us to invite certain individuals to be "part of us." We are trying not to be an elitist club, but we recognize that there are certain common denominators that do draw us together.

Today, Interprayer is known as the Interprayer International Partnership, with partners from three continents. Our principal value is friendship. We are firstly friends, and secondly leaders of prayer. Although we individually may be focused on one aspect of prayer or have links with other leaders and ministries, our connection with each other is important to all of us. We minister together whenever we can and we meet together twice a year – in America, Europe, or Africa! We are not alike; we are culturally diverse. But we are partnering together with a vision and desire to see the transformation of nations. And we have noticed that when we are together we receive what we can only describe as a "double anointing" – in other words, we are sharper and doubly effective in our joint ministry. We defer to one another and draw on each other's strengths, whilst compensating for each other's weaknesses.

Recently, God has started speaking to us about implementing corporately some of the things He is saying to us individually. A few are being led into areas of study and connection that are undoubtedly preparing them (and us) to be at the forefront of global issues and ministry. This partnership really works! We say we are "Praying together for Nations, Working together for Harvest."

For some years I was part of a leadership group called, appropriately, For England Together. Our desire was to encourage prayer ministries and individuals across England to stand "shoulder to shoulder" in prayer for change – at national and local level. Again, those of us involved were and are friends. A similar group exists within and for the British Isles and Ireland. These two groups have become committed to working together wherever we can and not being competitive.

Another partnership of prayer leaders that I have been part of is the International Prayer Council. This began its life in the year 2000 as the World Prayer Advisory Committee. Our first meeting of leaders, all of whom had some kind of profile and reputation in prayer ministry, took place in New York a few weeks after what has become known as "9/11" – the crashing of airliners into the twin towers of the World Trade Center in New York and into the Pentagon in Washington, DC. This grouping was driven by a sense of urgency. The world had changed, and we needed to get our act together.

Our focus is on the Great Commandment (loving God and our neighbor) and the Great Commission (going into all the world with the gospel). We too are looking for transformation of nations, and have helped to bring together a global network of ministries focused on transformation. We are also looking to see the strengthening of prayer throughout the world, which we have divided into fifteen identifiable regions, within which we are looking for the principal prayer mobilizers. Our first ever Global Consultation on Children in Prayer took place in 2006.

We seek to draw attention to some of the huge challenges facing us throughout the world, such as the 10/40 Window nations, the persecuted Church, the AIDS pandemic, global terrorism, and human disasters. Our aim is to get the Church and prayer movements more aware of the agenda for prayer, and to be together at the throne of grace.

We are looking for global partnering in prayer. So the annual Global Day of Prayer on Pentecost Sunday, preceded by ten days of prayer and fasting, and followed by ninety days of mercy ministry where we put feet on our prayers, has become our main annual organizational challenge, at least until 2010. We regularly issue "prayer connections" and "prayer alerts" to maintain a flow of information for prayer around the world, and are encouraging the development of regional hubs for disseminating such information into and from each region.[2] Through uniting with a common aim, several of us have become firm friends, and delight to do things together when we can. As an executive council we meet once a year and consult by conference calls every other month. We also consult with the regional leaders every year and maintain contact in between. We are big-picture people who are very much agenda driven, because the "love of Christ constrains us." We have a prayer shield of watchmen who also come together when we are in consultations together, and join us at some of our regional gatherings.

I believe that intentional partnerships in prayer are crucial and vital. Whether these operate on a local level, or around issues of common concern, or are concerned for national or international needs, it is essential that we all take prayer seriously. We can no longer look at prayer as something "*ad hoc.*" God's Word implores us to "be prepared in season and out of season." The early Church discovered the importance of *devoting* themselves to "the apostles' teaching and to the fellowship [partnership], to the breaking of bread *and to prayer*" (Acts 2:42, emphasis added). We cannot sit by and ignore what is happening around us. Through prayer, and through prayer with others, we can help bring change to individuals, communities, churches, and nations.

Notes

1. C. Peter Wagner, *Prayer Shield: How to Intercede for Pastors, Christian Leaders and Others on the Frontlines* (Regal, 1992).

2. Our website www.ipcprayer.org is worth visiting.

CHAPTER 18

TYPES OF PRAYER LEADERS

THE PRAYER MOVEMENT AROUND THE WORLD
has been described as "out of control"! That doesn't mean
that it is rebellious, but that it has grown so rapidly that no
one can keep pace with it or monitor it. Prayer meetings,
once described as "boring," are now among the most exciting of all Christian experiences. Prayer, once known as the
Cinderella of the Church, is producing the foot-soldiers of
the army of God.

There really has been a growth in all kinds of prayer
all round the world. The Body of Christ has discovered a
whole new world. Prayer has been released from the closet
and the Church onto the streets, into the hills, onto the
seas, and into the air – literally! People have traversed continents in prayer by walking and praying over many weeks.
People have climbed mountains to pray on the "high
places." People have hired planes to fly over cities to pray,
and even to anoint them with oil! People have hired boats
to sail around islands or along rivers in prayer. Others have
gone in bus or car journeys to pray. Some have walked and
prayed around the circumference of their city and around
the borders of their nation. Prayer teams have gone into

war zones and into other situations of conflict. Even Christians in persecuted areas of the world have learned about making up teams and going out in prayer into their own nation and neighboring nations. A new spirit of boldness has begun to grip the Church in many parts of the world. Prayer has been the lifeblood at the heart of some of the world's mega-churches. It has also been the key to some of the most amazing stories of church-planting movements, churches having been planted in some of the most unlikely places.

From the late 1980s through the 1990s millions of Christians around the globe engaged in Marches for Jesus in multiple centers. In the same time frame, huge stadia were hired in order to bring Christians together in prayer, since existing indoor arenas were too small to accommodate the numbers meeting together. Denominational barriers no longer seemed important; Christians reached out to one another to pray. Houses of prayer and large prayer centers have been established in many nations. Others have established prayer towers, both physical and spiritual ones. Mountains have been purchased and turned into twenty-four-hour prayer centers. There are even "prayer cities" where thousands of people have erected their homes around a prayer base in order to be nearby and involved daily. Some prisons have turned into twenty-four-hour prayer turbines! City-center squares, public parks, even beaches have been requisitioned for the people of God to gather together to pray. Some gatherings have run into millions of people in one place at the same time!

At the other end of the scale there has been an explosion of small-group prayer. Triplet groups, neighborhood groups, women's groups, businessmen's groups, children's groups – we are all becoming "groupies!" The macro-levels are matched and mirrored by the micro-levels of prayer, and so it should be. There's no value in us gathering for a big event once in a while, if we are not also gathering in small groups as often as we can.

Millions of children are part of this movement of prayer. There are even children's intercessory churches in some countries. In schools in many nations children gather around the flagpole, or kneel in the corridors and at the gates to pray. Youth prayer movements have "taken off like a rocket." "24/7 boiler rooms" have been established in many nations, manned mainly by young people. They are leading the rest of us in discovering and developing new, dynamic, creative ways of praying.

There are regular television and radio programs devoted to prayer. Many thousands of people telephone in for prayer. Documentaries have been made about prayer and reconciliation journeys. Prayer booths have been set up in market squares. Thousands of Christians regularly walk through their neighborhood in prayer. Regular calls to periods of prayer and fasting are issued the world over. At certain times of the year the Church around the world gathers in prayer in its millions. Prayer really is taking place around the throne of God, around the world, and around the clock.

Some amazing "prophetic acts" have characterized this prayer movement. As a consequence, walls have come down, gates and doors have opened, governments have toppled, reconciliation has taken place, and vast numbers have turned to Christ. Prayer is bringing about the huge changes that the promises in God's Word indicate are possible.

I have been immensely privileged to watch these developments and to be part of many of them. I haven't had time to be amazed but, to the uninformed or uninitiated onlooker, they must seem truly amazing. History will record in the years ahead what this means and what it will produce.

I guess, too, that some of our spiritual forebears are looking down from heaven in amazement at what is happening. It is to them that we owe a debt. For when things were tough and unyielding, they did not give up, but against hope continued to believe. Their prayers and writings, their example and perseverance have been an inspiration to those of us enjoying the fruit of what they prayed, did, and taught. I think of people like E.M. Bounds, Andrew Murray, Leonard Ravenhill, A.B. Simpson, A.W. Tozer, Rees Howells, and many, many more. "Thank you, Father, for the inspiration they have been."

New terminology has helped to define these new developments in prayer, and new kinds of leadership have emerged. For as new initiatives have been taken and new challenges have emerged, it has become necessary for this prayer to be "managed" and led well. But this has not been a man-managed movement. There is no overarching structure, no one significant leader. This has not been a top-down growth. There has been no "blueprint" to follow. The Spirit of God has been leading.

A few years ago Rachel Hickson and I were sharing in a DAWN national church-planting conference in Norway. We compared notes and found that we both had a similar list of current expressions that defined prayer leadership. Twenty years ago none of these would have been in existence, nor would they have been seen as necessary. These have all "emerged" as a response to the developments in prayer that I have described. Here are some of them.

- **Prayer mobilizers.** The passion of prayer mobilizers is to mobilize as many as possible within the denominations of the Church to learn about prayer and to be involved in prayer. Mobilizers want to take others with them on prayer assignments. Whether at city level or national level, they want to see more and more people catch fire for God and become involved in prayer. Prayer mobilizers are to be found at the micro-level as well as at the macro-level. These are the enthusiasts for prayer.

Their faith in what God can do in answer to prayer urges them to inspire others.

- **Prayer networkers**. The passion of networkers – whether for prayer or anything else in the Christian world – is to connect people of like vision and understanding together. Their delight is to introduce someone who is unaware of what is happening in their area of interest to others who are already active in that area, so as to prevent what we call "the reinvention of the wheel." They want to foster cooperation and eliminate competition. They know that unity is essential for effective prayer. So prayer networkers connect churches, prayer groups, and people of similar vision together in the same geographical area or around a common enterprise, theme, or vision.

- **Prophetic trumpet blowers**. These people are usually a step ahead of others, in that they see the issue that requires a rallying call. They are aware of God's timing to press forward in prayer. They usually have a keen awareness of God's voice prompting them. They are like the men of Issachar in King David's army, "who understood the times and knew what Israel should do" (1 Chronicles 12:32). They hear from heaven and give a lead on earth, rather like Nehemiah who galvanized the people of God to rebuild the broken down walls of Jerusalem, and to do so with prayer (see Nehemiah 4:9, 20).

- **Watchmen/Seers**. These are the leaders of praying troops who stand guard before God on behalf of their nation or city. Many of them spend hours in prayer, on their own or with others. Their leadership comes out of that experience. As they pray, they also gain understanding of impending danger and issue warnings to those with the ability to do something about it. They also see ahead, sounding the alarm and urging people to pray.

These also are ones who are watching what God is doing around the world, and who seek to listen to the Lord.

- **Teachers**. Teachers on prayer are those who want to unpack what the Scriptures say about prayer, and whose lives are given to train others in that understanding and in the practice of prayer. They hold prayer seminars and prayer schools. They seek to mix learning with doing. The Word of God is their textbook, the people of God their class, and the world around them is their laboratory. They will want us to pray as Jesus prayed, and with a similar passion to that of the early Church. They will want us to learn of the stalwarts of prayer in the Bible and of the classic prayers prayed in both Old and New Testaments.

- **Prayer researchers**. These people eat, breathe, and drink research. They want the praying community to be thoroughly aware of what we are up against, what the issues are, and what knowledge we need to inform us in praying. They are the ones to look at the history of a city, nation, or continent, and at the issues that Satan has used to maintain a stranglehold, either on the Church to prevent it being effective, or on the nation to prevent it being open to God.

- **Prayer administrators**. These may seem to have the least glamorous gift, but it is one of the most essential. Prayer administrators are at the heart of what goes on. They plan events, keep people informed, and share as much information as is wise to enable effective prayer. They work closely with prayer networkers and are the oil to keep the wheels of prayer turning. In my experience, alas, many with the gift of administration and a burden to pray end up wanting to pray more and administer less. So there is a dearth of people with the right skills to make everything happen effectively.

- **Prayer counselors**. Prayer counselors have a ministry to bring spiritual and physical healing to those individuals whose lives have been messed up by many things. These are the leaders whose motivation is to set people free from the tyranny of the evil one, so that they can take their place as effective members of the Body of Christ. They not only do the prayer counseling, but want to equip others to do it too. This area of ministry is a specialist one requiring both spiritual and secular qualifications, in order to keep within the laws of nations. Prayer counselors need to go beyond the obvious and to identify the hidden things of people's hearts, minds, emotions, and background.

- **Spiritual warfare leaders**. There is a danger in using this military term, since criticism is already being leveled at the Church for being too militaristic. However, these kinds of leaders exist and are necessary. They are the ones who have an understanding of the spiritual battleground, how Satan's kingdom is structured, what he is like, how he works, and the effective tactics to use to counteract his influence. They see not only the spiritual, behind-the-scenes activities of evil powers, but also become aware of the way the battle is being fought in the world around. They are alert to the Holy Spirit, and ensure that the prayer warriors are not foolhardy and unprotected but are equipped when it is time to do battle.

- **Breakthrough leaders**. Although similar to the former type of leader, there is a distinction. And there is a connection to the watchman or seer. Breakthrough leaders have a sense of the right time to press forward, where to concentrate their prayers, and what the immediate target is. They are unafraid of going into difficult and spiritually resistant territory. But they also know what the area of engagement should be and what to leave to another time. These are the ones to break open fast-closed doors and iron gates, and to bring an end to situations that have long defied resolution.

- **Assignment leaders**. There are many leaders to whom God seems to have given one area of life which is their prime area of responsibility in prayer. They are there as watchmen, but also have a responsibility to the rest of the Body of Christ. So part of what they do is to acquaint others with the facts and challenges. This could be for an age group (for example, children), an issue (such as AIDS, abortion, or the persecuted Church), a societal area (such as politics, Parliament, the legal profession, education, business, the media, or medicine), a people group (for example, the Buryats of Central Asia), a nation (such as Iraq), or a power bloc (such as the Islamic or Buddhist worlds). The knowledge and understanding they each have about their field is comprehensive and is needed by the Church when the time comes to focus prayer on their area of interest.

Even as I write, I am thinking about individuals who epitomize what each of these categories means. I can think of those that God has used extraordinarily within their gift-mix. None of these different categories need be singular. In my experience a prayer leader may have strengths in perhaps two of these areas. And although their concentration may be on one or two of these areas, that does not exclude them from operating in one of the others from time to time. Nor does this exclude them from praying. Far from it. Their leadership comes out of their praying.

I am also thinking of others who have become leaders of leaders, and people who write books, like this one, to challenge and equip others. But that could apply to every one of these categories of leaders. I'd like to see more writing on prayer by those who are doing exemplary and extraordinary things to advance the Kingdom of God. The rest of the Church needs to read the stories. I'd like to see many more visual resources telling the extraordinary stories of what God is doing around the world. Some of the best-kept secrets of God at work lie within the experience of those within the prayer movement. The rest of the Church needs to be challenged and equipped to pray so that they can help change their world.

God is a Creator. All the time, He is doing new things and presenting us with new challenges and opportunities. So, in time, this list may become out of date. Some leaders, like those in Scripture, have a mix of many or all of these gifts. Think of Moses. He was an intercessor, in that he sometimes spent days in God's presence. He knew when to exercise his authority in order to provide a way through the Red Sea. He also knew when to do some research by sending the spies into Canaan. He prayed on the high places at the time of battle, and he was the one to bring the tabernacle into existence as a place for the people to meet with God.

We know, too, that Jesus displayed all these praying qualities during His ministry on earth. We also know that He is still interceding in heaven and has been doing so for over 2,000 years! In fact, He "always lives to intercede" for us (Romans 8:34; Hebrews 7:25). He is in heaven "now to appear for us in God's presence" (Hebrews 9:24). So when we engage in intercession, we are joining in with the activity of Jesus in heaven. How awesome is that?!

CHAPTER 19

INTIMACY WITH THE FATHER

————————≈————————

ANYONE WHO WRITES ABOUT THIS SUBJECT is in danger of projecting himself as being superior. So, from the start, let me say that a greater intimacy with the Father is an objective I am still pursuing, and will probably continue to pursue until the day I die.

I know of no one who can say that they have achieved a close, intimate relationship with God in which they and God are fully satisfied. I do know of some who certainly have achieved a closer and more intimate relationship with God than I have. And I know of many who are longing with a deep desire to have a closer communion with the Father, the Son, and the Spirit.

Intimacy with the Father is something into which we all grow, and which we all need. I remember as a very young believer going with the rest of the youth group into the home of a bedridden and elderly person. At that time, her home was like a bit of heaven. Despite her restrictions she seemed to have an intimate relationship with God that pervaded her room. None of us wanted to leave her room. God was there.

A few years ago I met up with a fatherly church pastor in Connecticut, USA. His name was Dale Fife. We exchanged pleasantries as we sat at a meal table together. Then, in response to my question, he started to tell me how God had been speaking to him recently. The Holy Spirit had been drawing him into the presence of the Father. Each morning he had to go into his study and stay there for the whole day – not doing work, but waiting on God. Every day (except Sunday) for nine months, this had been going on. As he started to share with me, I became caught up with what he was sharing. And yet I sensed that even though he had spent nine months every day in God's presence, he was still only touching the hem of His garment, so to speak.

He told me how out of that experience of "the presence" and of communion with Him, God had given him five books to write. His first one had just been published, called *The Secret Place*.[1] Every page breathed a reality of God's presence that I knew I did not have. It read like an allegory as God took him on a spiritual journey, showing him things that one can only describe as beyond this earthly realm and therefore truly prophetic. At no time did I feel he was bragging. On the contrary, his sharing acted as a spur to me. A deep longing developed within me for something similar.

That longing is still there. Only occasionally has that longing begun to find fulfillment. And when it has, it has resulted in me being taken beyond anywhere I had spiritually been before. Several of my friends have a similar longing. Some of them have made regular provision in their busy lifestyle to spend time in God's presence. Businessmen visit city-center churches for thirty minutes at lunchtime every day for quiet, reflective prayer. Christian workers spend a day or more every month at a retreat center or monastery, just being quiet in God's presence, and sometimes being subject to spiritual guides who will teach them about the practicalities of being in God's presence and of the gift of silence.

In ancient Egypt the Desert Fathers used to congregate at monasteries in the desert between Cairo and Alexandria to seek God and to wait before Him. Some would spend most of their lives doing that. And they still do. In fact, that experience of seeking God and being in His presence has been a shared value of many of the Coptic Orthodox priests. I met one of these men a couple of years ago. He was probably half my age, but he had wisdom and a sense of "the presence" that exuded from a deep relationship with God and which reflected in him an awesome appetite for more of the same.

Jesus in prayer

Why did Jesus spend hours in prayer? Surely He had an unbroken relationship with the One He termed "your Father and my Father"? However, the Gospel writer Luke records twelve occasions when Jesus is praying. Sometimes that praying was heard or noticed by others. At other times Jesus was by Himself.

Heaven was open to Him at His baptism (Luke 3:21), and thereafter Jesus had an open heaven in prayer. After that, He was led for forty days of fasting and prayer into the desert, where He was tempted by the devil (Luke 4:1–2). Thereafter, Jesus often withdrew to lonely places and prayed (Luke 5:16). He went out onto the mountainside to pray all night (Luke 6:12). Once, He took Peter, James and John with Him up a mountain to pray (Luke 9:28–36). At that time, He met with God, heard His voice and became transfigured (literally, "metamorphosed"), as his face and garments shone with a bright light. He also met and talked with Moses and Elijah – both of them had lived on earth many hundreds of years previously and yet were here appearing to Jesus.

At other times the rest of His disciples were also with Him as He prayed. Luke 9:18 tells us that He was once praying in private, but His disciples were with Him. And in Luke 11:1 we read, "One day Jesus was praying in a certain place." When He finished, the disciples asked Him to teach them to pray. So, even though it was an intensely private occasion for Jesus, the disciples could sense something significant was going on.

The climax of Jesus' prayer was in the Garden of Gethsemane (see Luke 22:39–46). The three disciples were with Him again, but for Jesus this time His prayer was intimate, lonely, and all-consuming.

> Being in anguish He prayed more earnestly, and his sweat was like drops of blood falling to the ground.
>
> (Luke 22:44)

The spiritual battle in advance of the cross was being fought. We say He was travailing in prayer. But this was a travail that none of us has ever experienced. Then, on the cross, He prayed the greatest prayer that has ever been prayed, "Father, forgive them," and then He handed Himself over to God.

So we see, through the experience of Jesus, both the ecstasy and the agony that prayer can be: ecstasy on the mountain when He was transfigured, and agony in the garden where He travailed.

When we know the Father and have an intimate relationship with Him, then we can at times travail in prayer. Some of the needs in the world around us require travailing prayer in order to achieve breakthrough. We will never see radical change until we are able to agonize, travail and, in prolonged prayer, pour out our hearts to God. We need to intercede as Jesus did. Travail is a product of desperation to see things change. Similarly, to enjoy intimacy with the Father requires desperation on our part. We need to hunger and thirst after Him, after His righteousness and His holiness. In order to do that, we need to starve other things!

That's what *we* need. But the Father Himself looks for that close fellowship with us too. The Father is seeking the right kind of worshippers (John 4:23). Jesus wants us to see and share the Father's glory (John 17:24). He wants us to experience the Father's love (John 14:15, 21, 23). All that Jesus enjoyed in His relationship with His Father He has bequeathed to us also.

> All that belongs to the Father is mine. That is why I said the Spirit will take from what is mine and make it known to you.
>
> (John 16:15)

How much of that have we individually gleaned? Have we even begun to enter into the kind of intimacy with the Father that Jesus enjoyed?

The holy of holies

Some years ago I was meeting with other British prayer leaders for our annual conference. There were about thirty or forty of us together, and we met somewhere in the Midlands of England. During a time of waiting on God together, I sensed that God was drawing us deeper into His presence, and this was expressed through a very strong mental/spiritual revelation. We were being led into the sanctuary of the temple of God – into the "holy of holies."

In the Spirit (and in my mind), we were being led through the outer court of the temple (the place to meet with God). There was much activity and bustle as people carried on with what they were doing, paying no attention to us. Then we came to the inner court (the holy place), where studiously several people were seated at desks, poring over the Scriptures. Here was a place of study, of engagement

with God's written Word. Again no one seemed to notice us
as we passed through.

Finally we were led into the inner sanctuary. As we
passed through the doorway into this, the holy of holies, we
had to take off our shoes. As we did so, we became aware of
the presence of God and of Jesus. We also became acutely
aware of our own ill-preparedness. We were no longer
observers of what others were doing; we were now par-
ticipators. The Lord said to us, "Take off your garments."
The outer garment looked reasonably clean, but the under-
garments became progressively dirtier. The dirty garments
were taken from us one by one as we disrobed.

As each garment began to be taken off, I was flat on my
face, weeping. The problem was that I was unaware of this
filth. I thought I was outwardly respectable. But inwardly I
was, oh, so needy. Eventually our nakedness was obvious,
although we didn't see each other; we saw only ourselves. I
felt embarrassed, vulnerable, laid bare, with no pretense, no
covering, and unable to hide.

Then, after what seemed an age of lonely awareness of
how we were – sinful, dirty, and unworthy – the Lord went
behind a screen and brought out for each of us a new, white,
clean robe. He told us to stand up and put them on. Once
those robes were on, only then were we in a fit state to worship Him, to be with Him, and enjoy His fellowship.

After spending some time in the holy of holies, Jesus led
us out back through the way we had come in. This time,
however, the atmosphere had changed. As He entered the
place of study, everyone stood up, smiled, and followed us
out in procession into the outer court. There the busy-ness
had ceased and everyone was waiting, and they cheered and
praised as we followed Jesus out. All eyes were on Him.

I have pondered this revelation many times, and each
time the most significant part was always the encounter in
the holy of holies. We have to go through the process of

being made holy – again – if we are to enjoy true communion with God. Busy-ness in God's service, having busy
lifestyles, even being busy with the study of God's Word, is
not the reality. My being without any encumbrance is what
He requires, and is the prerequisite for close fellowship with
Him. So, intimacy with the Father starts with clean hands
and a pure heart (see Psalm 24:4). Then I may stand in His
holy place. Then I can ascend the hill of the Lord.

Being in the throne room

At another time I was on my own in prayer; it may have
been at night – most of what I would term "significant
revelation" comes during the night seasons! This time it
was a kind of vision of being taken into the throne room
of God.

Going into a throne room of a sovereign or head of state
is pretty significant. Those who do so remember it for the
rest of their lives. Usually it is a one-off experience, unless
you happen to be among the privileged few whose task it is
to be in and out of the throne room on a daily basis. When
Queen Esther went into the throne room she, even though
she was a wife of King Xerxes, was unsure of the reception
she would receive. Anyone who approached uninvited could
be put to death (see Esther 4:11–14; 5:1–2)!

Strangely, I did not feel that my entry into God's throne
room was exceptional or one-off. I felt I could go into it
whenever I wished. Hebrews 4:16 and 10:19–22 support
this. As I approached the throne room, the guards (probably angels) stood aside and opened the door for me. It
was as if I was expected. I hope I had the right garment on!
As I entered the throne room, the crowds that were inside
made a path for me so that I could approach the throne
on which was seated our God, surrounded by those who
attended Him.

I had no fear in coming to Him. I wasn't aware of my sin; that had been dealt with. I felt welcome as I walked forward. My eyes were on Him, not on the crowds around Him. I was oblivious to the angels or to the surroundings. It was His presence I had come into. The others were there by right, of course, but it was Him I had come to see and worship.

As I approached the throne, God beckoned me to His side. Then I thought, Is this God or is it Jesus? Jesus is seated on the throne too. I didn't get an answer, and I suppose I didn't need to know since the two are as one. The significant thing was that I didn't see two thrones, only one.

However, once I was by the side of Him who sat upon the throne, He said to me, "Turn around. Look and see what I see." As I turned and looked, I realized I was seeing, through His eyes, the world in all its need. It was merely a glimpse. But in that moment, I sensed this was the place of intercession. We needed to intercede with what the One on the throne saw. We needed His understanding, His will, and His compassion surging through us. The words from Ephesians 2:6–7 came to mind:

> And God raised us up with Christ, and seated us with him in the heavenly realms in Christ Jesus, in order that in the coming ages he might show ...

We need a heavenly perspective on earthly situations, if ever the prayer of Jesus is to be answered:

> Your kingdom come,
> your will be done
>> on earth as it is in heaven.

(Matthew 6:10)

I cannot merely pray from my human knowledge and understanding. It will always be incomplete, narrow, one-sided, and even biased. I need to know God's mind and heart about the situations on earth that He wishes to change.

So, for me, my visit to the throne room was not a one-off. It wasn't so that I could recall the glory of what I had witnessed. It was for me to understand that I needed God's perspective for effective prayer. Of course, being with Him and beholding His glory is still a longing – one that will take eternity to fulfill. Being in the place where I can enjoy His presence is a continuing longing too.

But I have learned that spending time in His presence can have a variety of purposes. I need that for myself. God needs it for Himself; after all, we are in relationship. But I also need to be in His presence for greater effectiveness in His service and in prayer. I need to hear His voice, again and again, speaking to me about what He sees and knows, and what He wishes to pray. I have learned that prayer is not so much a human activity in which I invite God to listen to me. It is a divine activity in which I join. God the Father is listening to the Son who is interceding continuously. He is also listening to the Holy Spirit who sometimes interprets the heart of Father God to us via groans, tears, and anguish as He intercedes for us, through us, and with us (see Romans 8:26–27).

Several of those working among children, helping them with prayer and intercession, have told me, "The children love to lie in God's presence and listen to what He wants to tell them." Do you? Do I? Do we? Does the Church?

Notes

1. Dale Arthur Fife, *The Secret Place: Passionately Pursuing His Presence* (Whitaker House, 2001).

CHAPTER 20

AN ARMY OF INTERCESSORS

$\approx$

SOME YEARS AGO MY WIFE AND I visited the city of Goiania in Brazil. At the time, Elizabeth Cornelio and Elizabeth Albernaz were leading a remarkable prayer ministry among women in the city. They had a prayer tower which served as an office for the ministry and a base for training intercessors. Through a radio program they had communication with 30,000 intercessors in the state of Goias. Their links with both church and city leadership was strong. The churches were strong and growing, and they were experiencing what I understand to be a classic revival.

They were in communication with the police and fire service, who would inform them about their fight against crime. Prayer for every section of the city and state had been developed, and the intercessors would go into action whenever a call was made. In this way crime began to fall. Eventually these two women were given an award by the city leaders, in recognition of the changes that had occurred through their leadership in prayer.

These intercessors were being trained into an army, not a physical one with physical weapons but a spiritual army using spiritual weaponry. It was fascinating watching them in action. In some churches in which I was preaching, there would be a group of intercessors on the platform, praying for the leaders and speakers. Others were assigned to stand around the auditorium at even distance from one another, praying for the people and the effect of God's Word. Every church had a prayer coordinator, whose task was to lead prayer gatherings every day.

"Would you pray for our intercessory leaders, please?" one pastor asked me.

"How many do you have?" I asked.

"Three," he replied, as he introduced me to three twenty-year-old young men!

"How often do you lead prayer?" I asked.

"Every day" was the answer! "This one leads at 6 a.m., this one at 12 noon, and this one at 6 p.m."

I felt they should be praying for me.

Every Friday night was recognized as a night of prayer across the city. One Friday, we attended five separate prayer gatherings during the night. Three thousand praying folk would gather on a hill overlooking the city. Others gathered in hotels and large churches to pray. On another occasion 20,000 Christians met together in a football stadium for a night of prayer, culminating at 5.30 a.m. in a dawn march into the city center to claim the city for Christ and His Kingdom. These intercessors wanted to make a difference to their city, even though it had been designed and dedicated to the Masonic!

Redefining intercession

In my country, "intercessors" seem to be regarded with caution, if not suspicion. Often they are viewed as elitist people or groups. Why is that? Is it because most Christians, even leaders, do not fully understand what intercession is all about? Do they see it as the same as prayer? Or are they put off by the other-worldliness sometimes portrayed by those who talk about interceding?

Whatever the answer, it is wrong to throw out the baby of intercession with the bathwater of misunderstanding. Intercession is a Biblical word. It is linked to prayer and is a development from prayer.

The word translated as "intercession" in the Greek (New Testament) and Hebrew (Old Testament) is always different from the other words used to describe prayer. The Greek word *entugchano* literally means "to entreat," or "to make a plea." Sometimes it is used with the preposition *huper*, meaning "on behalf of someone," as in Romans 8:26 when the Spirit makes intercession *for us*. Only once in the New Testament is this Greek word translated as "prayer" – that is, in 1 Timothy 4:5. It seems strange that it is, yet from verse 1 it seems that Paul is implying the work of the Spirit in what follows. Everywhere else in the New Testament, this word is used in connection with prayer that comes from Jesus, the Great High Priest, or from the Holy Spirit. There is a divine component or connection to it, as in Romans 8:26, 27, and 34, and in Hebrews 7:25. It is used to describe the prayer of Jesus or of the Holy Spirit. Does this mean, then, that we shouldn't apply it to ourselves? No, for in 1 Timothy 2:1, Paul writes:

> I urge, then, first of all, that requests, prayers, intercession [*entugchano*] and thanksgiving be made for everyone.

The implication is that all of us can engage in intercession, if we understand what it truly is, and how the Godhead is involved with us in this type of prayer. The prominent thought is that of boldness and freedom in approach to God.[1]

The Hebrew word translated as "intercession" is always *paga*, meaning "to cause to entreat" or "to intercede." It is used prophetically of Jesus in Isaiah 53:12:

> He ... was numbered with the transgressors.
> For He bore the sin of many,
> > and made intercession [*paga*] for the transgressors.

It is also used in Jeremiah 7:16 in the words of God to Jeremiah:

> Do not ... offer any plea [*paga*] or petition for them ... for I will not listen.

In both cases, the word relates to the way God sees intercession as being concerned with pleading before Him on behalf of others. In Jeremiah 27:18, the prophet is speaking about other prophets hearing from God and having the word of the Lord, then says,

> Let them plead [*paga*] with the LORD Almighty.

Again there is a divine component; they have heard from heaven first, before they intercede.

It is that awareness of the will of God, of having heard from God, coupled with a willingness to plead on behalf of someone or a group of people, that constitutes intercession as God sees it.

Put simply, intercession is *prayer that originates in heaven and is taken back to God in expectation of an answer*. Each of these examples reflects the importance and significance of having heard from God first before true intercession (*paga*) could occur.

Intercession is more than ordinary prayer. It is us and God in harmony in prayer. It is us being bold and free in His presence. It is us making a plea before God, knowing the rightness of our cause. It us praying with the Word of

God and with the knowledge of what is His will. The kind of intercession God is looking for is very often accompanied by copious tears, as I describe in Chapter 14. God seems to communicate His feelings through us as we pray. It is therefore us, made in God's own image, being so in tune with Him that we are truly praying the prayers of heaven.

In Isaiah 59, the prophet describes the situation in the nation among the people. Hands are stained with blood; lips have spoken lies; acts of violence are in their hands; feet are swift to shed innocent blood; and justice is far removed. In fact the absence of justice overrides the sins committed. No one calls for justice; there is no justice in their paths. "So justice is far from us ... We look for justice but find none ... justice is driven back," complains Isaiah (verses 4, 8, 9, 11 and 14). As God looks at this situation – and also, may we say, similar ones – He sees that "there was no-one, he was appalled that there was no-one to intervene [*paga*]" (verse 16). The Authorized Version puts it:

He ... wondered that there was no intercessor.

In such situations of devastation God is looking for those who will intercede. He didn't say there was *no* prayer – He was looking for *more*. He was looking for intercession. He was looking for someone who was prepared to stand in the gap to turn things around, and to pray feelingly and pleadingly. He was looking for someone who wouldn't ignore the sin, but rather would be able to identify with the sins of the people, and pray with the anguish needed – as His Son did centuries later. He was, in short, looking for someone to pray in partnership with Himself.

So God stepped in. In verses reminiscent of Ephesians 6 (the "armor" verses), He donned the garb to enable Him to work salvation and be sustained by righteousness.

As God looks at our world, He is not looking primarily for more prayer, but for more of the right kind of prayer. He is looking for watchmen to be on guard, to watch and pray – a theme that is echoed in Isaiah (see 52:8; 56:10; 62:6), in Jeremiah (see 6:17; 31:6), and in Ezekiel (see 3:17; 22:30; 33:7). In each case it is God Himself Who is speaking. So we had better listen!

The idea of watchmen in prayer would be familiar to the Jews. Every city was distinguished by the fact that it had a wall surrounding it. Some cities were quite small, unlike cities of today. The wall was there to protect. On each wall were watchtowers, spaced at even distances or strategic points around the city. The inhabitants knew the importance of mounting a twenty-four-hour-a-day watch from those watchtowers. Their safety and survival depended on those watchmen being alert and doing their job properly.

So it is with intercession. God is looking for twenty-four-hour-a-day watchmen who will watch, pray, guard, and intercede. The watchmen God wants need to be committed to be on guard at their appointed and agreed times. Their area of responsibility can be for their street, their neighborhood, their city, or their nation. I cannot stress enough the importance God attaches to this area of ministry – this calling in prayer. He is calling us into the spiritual battle zone.

I heard of one lady who had committed herself to God to pray for her street and her neighbors. One night, as she prayed before going to bed, she felt it very important to continue in prayer beyond midnight, although she didn't know why. The next day she discovered that, overnight, there had been ten attempted burglaries in her street, but none of them had succeeded. Her prayers, on this occasion, provided physical protection, as she remained on guard spiritually.

Intercessors are a vital part of any community of Christians. In Western churches they tend to be seen as a minority group. So, little notice is taken of them. My heart is to see that small group become a big group. I think we have too few committed to intercede. Too few prepared to be watchmen for their community. Too few praying – really praying – for their nation. Too few who believe that God can answer big prayers for things to change. Too few who understand the nature of true intercession. Too few prepared to be committed to pray as God intended. We need an army of intercessors.

Preparing the army

So where do we start? The challenge is to turn people who pray, however spasmodically, however limited the experience of prayer, and at whatever level, into warriors of prayer. Most Christians pray. They may not pray for a long time. They may not pray daily. They may not know how to "pray without ceasing." They may be used to praying only about personal things, or for family members. They may cry out to God only when facing a personal crisis. But we can build on all that.

I can well imagine that in East Germany the handful of Christians who gathered every Monday evening throughout the 1980s to pray, in the churches of Leipzig, never dreamed that at the end of the decade they would see the fruit of those prayers in a changed government and the demolition of the Berlin Wall. I have no idea whether they prayed with much faith or little faith. But I do know that thousands of others around the world were also praying at the same time for the penetration of the communist bloc with the gospel. I know of individuals who, when visiting Berlin, would go to the wall to pray for it to fall, and for the people behind it to be set free. I know of a youth group who went to their pastor and said, "God has told us we should be praying for the breaking down of the Berlin Wall and the reunification of Germany." They too went to the wall to pray – at the precise place where two weeks later the first bulldozer came to demolish the wall. Different parts of this story of sudden change have been told in several books. We'll have to wait until eternity to find out the full, unabridged version!

God, who "set eternity in the hearts of men" (Ecclesiastes 3:11), had set the same burden for change in the hearts of men and women in many nations. At whatever level they prayed, their prayers met at the throne of grace. God heard and answered.

In Romania in 1989, thousands of people gathered in the squares of some of the cities, such as Oradea. The media portrayed them as protesters, but we now know they were mostly Christians who met to pray. Their prayers helped to bring to an end the ruthless dictatorship of Nicolai Ceausescu.

Then, in 2004–05 there was an "orange revolution" in Kiev, Ukraine. That too was a prayer-based revolution. Those the media showed as being on the streets were mostly Christians, praying against injustice and for change.

These examples illustrate that Christians can gather around a common theme and at a crucial time to pray, even beyond their faith. And God, from heaven, inspires His children and orchestrates their coming together amidst a rising crescendo of believing prayer.

But there's another way. God sometimes speaks through dreams, as he did to Jacob (Genesis 28:12) and Joseph (Genesis 37:5). He also spoke to Nebuchadnezzar in a dream (Daniel 2:1), to which Daniel obtained the interpretation (after a night of prayer). Pilate's wife also had a dream (Matthew 27:19). And God told the prophet Joel that He would pour out His Spirit on all people and "your old men will dream dreams" (Joel 2:28). I have even met some people who have seen Jesus in their dreams and have been converted through dreams! I have friends who have a ministry in dream interpretation and dream psychology, so there is something in our dreams – at least some of them – that is worth taking note of.

I am not a dreamy person, so when I have a dream that I remember, it is noteworthy. But to have the same dream three nights running is, for me, extremely rare – in fact previously unknown. In one dream (which I had in March 2006) I was being shown by Dr Billy Graham around orphanages that he had established. And I was saying, "Billy, this is a wonderful legacy you have left." Why Billy Graham? I had worked with him during Mission England and the Mission to London in the 1980s. But I had had no meeting with him for many years, nor do I know if he has established any orphanages.

On the third occasion, as I seemed to re-enter the world of the subconscious, I sensed I was saying, "Why am I being shown around these places, and what does this mean?"

Then God said, "This is for you." Then I sensed God was saying that we in the ministry I belong to – the Interprayer International Partnership – need to establish orphanages in each country where we are from and in which we work. Unlike most orphanages, however, these are not merely to be caring establishments to look after orphans. They are also to be places where the children are taught how to live a life of faith, hear from God, pray, evangelize, and plant churches. The children are to be hand-picked as we look for those on whom God already has His hand. They are to be young teenagers (ten to fourteen years old). They are to be given a vision for the future so that, by the time they are ready to leave the orphanage, they have a life vision and are equipped to go and make things happen in the nations. They are to be the future "nation changers." I also sensed that in countries such as Uganda, Malawi, and Brazil (in which some of my colleagues already work) this can happen more readily, because of the huge needs. But we also need to establish such ministries to orphans in Western nations.

In September 2006 I attended the first Global Consultation on Children in Prayer, hosted by the International Prayer Council, in Malaysia. Among the topics shared by many practitioners from more than forty nations represented, the theme of orphanages occurred many times. What I found surprising and immensely encouraging was that in many of these situations the word that God had given me about orphanages was already being worked out. The young were already being equipped to live by faith, pray, and plant churches.

Can it be that God wants to raise an army of intercessors out of the "fatherless generation"? Can it be that He wants to teach the young-in-years more about intercession and living by faith than has been learned by those who are two, three, or four times their age? It is just like God to pick those whom the world regards as deprived and as "problem people" to produce quality Christians, with a quality of faith and an understanding of intercession. It is just like Him to equip a generation who will be so in touch with their heavenly Father that the absence of earthly fathers pales into insignificance alongside the care that He can give them. And it is just like Him to be in such relationship with them that they are instinctively able to hear His voice and go and do His will. "Lord, make us willing to be the channels you can use to bring this about."

God wants us to soar with Him in the heavenlies. Just as an eagle catches the thermals and soars into the heavens, God wants us to catch the wind of His Spirit and rise up "on wings like eagles" as we wait upon Him (Isaiah 40:31). An eagle sees from above. Other creatures see from the earth. God wants us to be praying from His viewpoint on high, and not merely from the immediacy of our earthly perspective. He wants to increase our faith in what He can do, instead of us being preoccupied with what we can do.

Doubt sees the obstacles, faith sees the way,
Doubt sees the darkest night, faith sees the day,
Doubt plumbs the deepest depths, faith soars on high,
Doubt questions, "Who believes?" Faith answers, "I."[2]

Notes

1. Interlinear Greek–English New Testament comment on synonyms.

2. Author unknown.

CHAPTER 21

DREAM AND CHANGE
YOUR NATION

―――――――――― ≈ ――――――――――

*I*MAGINE WHAT IT WOULD BE LIKE to be in a situation where:

- the tangible presence of God was being frequently experienced

- peace and harmony reigned on our streets

- crime of all kinds was declining

- social problems were diminishing

- the media was taking notice of what God was doing, both in society and in the Church

Imagine, and ask God, "Can this be? Here, in Britain?" And if so, what will it take to turn things around and begin the process?

As I was meeting with my secretary on the morning of 7 July 2005 for prayer and business discussion, God started to speak to me about towers of praise and prayer around the coasts of Great Britain and of a call for seven years of prayer. We were in the UK prayer room of the Ashburnham prayer center at the time. It seemed somewhat incongruous. Here we were, trying to major on business matters, when the Holy Spirit was downloading into my spirit what turned out to be a call to pray for the nation. Every time we stopped talking and began praying – about the business matters we were discussing – I was getting a bit more of the picture about this strategy of prayer.

The vision

During our times of prayer that morning, God said to me three times, "London is vulnerable." I believe He was saying this in relation to the lack of strategic prayer there, and therefore the lack of His presence.

He was also saying that we needed to link prayer together around the coast of Britain to provide a protective spiritual barrier, particularly at the gateway towns. I was seeing these towers: they were like tall buildings, of differing heights, side by side around the coastline. They were to be towers of prayer and praise, created by God's people coming together and standing together, "shoulder to shoulder" (see Zephaniah 3:9). The differing heights reflected different levels of praying. What seemed to be important was not our understanding or volume of prayer and praise, but our commitment to begin to bring this about.

In effect, the Spirit was saying that it was time to get really serious about:

- the protection of our nation spiritually
- the preparing of the way, both for us who live in Britain and for the people of the world who will visit Britain, to come into God's presence
- the transformation of our nation

Later that morning, and after our meeting, we found out that several suicide bombers had exploded bombs on the London Underground and on a double-decker bus, causing hundreds of casualties, scores of deaths, mayhem in London, and sending shock waves around the world. The leaders of the G8 nations were at that time meeting in Scotland, so the eyes of the world were on the nation in a way that rarely happens. Suddenly, the time we spent in prayer that morning took on major significance.

Since then, Britain has had more attempted bombings and seen multiple cells of Islamic fundamentalist terrorists arrested. We have also seen how vulnerable London and the nation really are to the terrorist threat. So the question that God seemed to be putting to me was, "Where is the spiritual protection for London and Britain?" We are vulnerable to attack. But we, as God's people, have a vital role to fulfill.

I also strongly felt that God was saying it would take seven years of prayer to bring about a spiritual climate change in the nation. We had seven years to bring this about; seven years to mobilize prayer. We (that is, Christian leaders throughout the country) had to motivate, mobilize, organize, connect, focus, and increase the level of praying as much as possible through a coordinated strategy.

God had been speaking to others about this too, and that encouraged me. When He is serious about something changing, He usually doesn't speak just to one person but to many about the same thing. He had begun to say to different people that we had a seven-year window to turn things around. Seven years to:

- mobilize prayer and lift up the name of the Lord
- establish "towers of praise" around our coasts
- connect the Body of Christ together in our towns and villages to praise and worship Him, and beseech Him for a fundamental change in our society and nation

- prepare this nation spiritually
- begin to make a difference

At the time of writing, this means that we now have less than three years to complete this task. In the providence of God the level of prayer has begun to rise in many ways and in many places. Prayer centers have been established in many places, and people have been walking and praying over their stretch of the coast or around the borders of their county. Some have even moved house to be in a strategic place of prayer. God has raised up a wonderful brother – Jonathan Oloyede from Nigeria – who has stimulated continuous prayer in the London boroughs and has also brought Christians together across the capital for Global Day of Prayer events since 2006.

This word was also relevant because of the 2012 Olympics, due to be held in Britain. The awarding of the Olympics to London had been announced just one day before the bombings. I have no doubt that security considerations will be on the agenda as the Sports Council and the government prepare for the Olympics.

But God was interested in something different. He wanted us, His people, to prepare also. His presence is to be prevalent in our nation and experienced in every area of life. That presence is to be tangible, and experienced as an "open heaven." So, when athletes from around the world, together with the world's media and thousands of spectators, come here for the Olympics, what they would begin to find was a nation where the presence of God was apparent. They would find that we, as God's people, were ready to welcome them into the presence of God, as well as into our nation.

People from the nations of the world will be coming to Britain. Many of those nations have been victims of injustice, unfair trade, and political mishandling. Many of those nations have something against us. But out of an attitude of humility and love, here will be a chance for us to come in the opposite spirit of all that. This is a golden opportunity for us to bless them, whatever their ethnic origin, belief, language, and social status. To prepare the way for the Church to welcome them with love, grace, charm, politeness, and with a positive message born out of God's love in our hearts. Isn't that worth praying for?

Interestingly, two items on television in July 2005 encouraged me. BBC South East news carried a report about a young man named Gary Lamb who had just completed a prayer walk around the entire coast of Britain! It had taken him two years to do it, with the support of his church and his family. He was a kind of John the Baptist, a forerunner of what God had been showing me.

In the same month BBC2 television started screening a series of programs, titled simply *Coast*, on the coastline around Britain. This series proved to be so popular and such compelling viewing that it has been repeated again and again, either in whole or in part. I have felt that these showings have in their way been prophetic! All around our coasts are buildings – castles, keeps, towers, forts – constructed for the nation's defense against attack.

The first program in the series focused on the coast between Dover and Exmouth, stating that this is the frontline in our nation's defense.

- Dover – the place symbolizing the Second World War's Battle of Britain by air.

- Folkestone (and along the coast) – where seventy-two Martello towers were built 200 years ago for protection!

- Dunge – where a unique early-warning system of air attack had been established more than sixty years ago.

- Hastings and Pevensey – the places where William the Conqueror landed in 1066 and the Norman invasion began (the last time England was successfully invaded and conquered). These ports and twelve others are regarded as cinque ports – the first in line for England's defense.

- Portsmouth – the place from which the navy set sail for the Battle of Trafalgar and one of the principal bases for the naval defenses of the two twentieth-century world wars.

- The Channel Islands – where the German occupation of the Second World War succeeded.

- Weymouth – where the black plague, responsible for the death of millions, first entered the country.

I live near the East Sussex coast. Here, as in many other areas around our coast, smuggling has been rife for centuries; the latest wave is of illegal immigrants and illicit drugs. Because we are an island nation, many wish to come here to live and work, looking for the good life, or looking to gain advantage from our vulnerability.

The policing of our borders happens to be a current political talking point. We are still vulnerable to invasions of many kinds. We are also extremely vulnerable spiritually. Has there ever been any attempt to provide spiritual protection for our nation? Was God saying something more to us, by the "coincidence" of these television programs? Isn't it time to put something in place?

What will that strategy begin to look like?

We need to mobilize prayer and engage in prayer on a higher level than ever before in a coordinated fashion in and around the Greater London area. London is still vulnerable.

What prayer is taking place? How strategic is it? Are there gaps in the wall of prayer around the M25 London ring road? Are the London borough connections firmly established? Christians need to cooperate and join in prayer across the denominational, racial, linguistic, and cultural barriers. I am glad to say that this has already begun to happen in a coordinated way.

We need to see strategic prayer and praise in all the coastal gateways of Great Britain. This too has begun to happen.

We need to look for a "welcome event" for Christians from our former Empire nations, either ahead of or in connection with the Olympics in 2012.

We need to link in with the Global Day of Prayer and other national and international prayer calls between now and 2012, so that we look towards a gathering momentum of prayer throughout Great Britain.

Quality of praise and prayer: the Biblical example

During this period of time (before and after July 2005) God had also been speaking to me about the importance of gatekeepers and watchmen. We normally regard pastors in cities and towns as "gatekeepers." However, in Biblical times, the city elders sat at the gates of cities to discuss and make decisions, but they weren't guardians of the city. That was the task of watchmen.

However, Biblically, gatekeepers have another function. They are not principally pastors of churches and leaders of cities, but are the folk with spiritual responsibility to worship the Lord and to guard the place where God's presence is to be experienced. The gatekeeping defined in 1 Chronicles 9:17–33 was in the context of bringing back the ark of God (and therefore of His presence) into Jerusalem.

The gatekeepers were chosen from among the Levites, the priestly tribe. They were responsible for guarding the thresholds of the Tent of Meeting and then the house of the Lord. They were assigned to particular locations, on the north, south, east, and west, by night and by day. Some had responsibility for practical elements of worship; others were to be musicians and had to stay in the temple! Their role was highly significant in maintaining the spiritual atmosphere for the presence of God to be experienced by all who entered.

In 1 Chronicles 14:11–15, God "breaks out" against his enemies at Baal Perazim and says:

> As soon as you hear the sound of marching in the tops of the balsam trees, move out to battle.
>
> (verse 15)

The Philistines were defeated, and their gods were burned! The strategy we adopt has to be led from heaven! Only God will enable us to break through!

In 1 Chronicles 15 and 16 the ark is brought to Jerusalem in the appointed and correct way. Gatekeepers feature in this (15:18, 23–24). The psalm of David was given to Asaph and his fellow gatekeepers (16:7–36), as probably many of the psalms in Scripture were.

The gatekeepers were to stand as guards over the ark of God's presence, and were to present offerings twice a day, and give thanks to the Lord with trumpets, cymbals, and other instruments (16:37–42).

According to 1 Chronicles 23:5 approximately 9 percent of the Levites committed to rebuilding the temple were to be involved as gatekeepers and 9 percent in praising the Lord. So there was a twin function in both praise and worship, and in guardianship. There were praising gatekeepers and practical gatekeepers. In 1 Chronicles 25:1, some of the gatekeepers had a ministry of prophesying. The divisions of the gatekeepers are recorded in 1 Chronicles 26, and in the second part of verse 16 we get this marvelous verse which links in with Zephaniah 3:9:

> Guard was alongside guard.
>
> (1 Chronicles 26:16)

In other words, they had to stand together. Unity was vital.

We need such gatekeepers, devoted to praise and worship, to be released and developed as part of the strategy of prayer around the coasts and in London, in addition to the watchmen intercessors who are in place already. Watchmen are primarily to be occupied with the guardianship of the city or nation (and even streets and villages). Their role is to provide a twenty-four-hour watch spiritually, both against the intrusion of unwanted and alien influences, and for the people going about their daily business. They are to give warnings to the leaders. When both watchmen and gatekeepers are significantly and purposefully in place, this will help to increase the level of praying, even into the heavens! The objective is to prepare the way for the presence of God to be experienced, not in one place such as a temple, but throughout the nation! What a challenge!

So far in this chapter, I have spoken solely about Britain. I dream of seeing a different Britain. I dream of experiencing the tangible presence of God in many, many places around Britain. I want to see this nation change. I want to see trends reversed. I want to see more of God at work and less of Satan at work. I want to see people coming to faith in Christ from every walk of life, every stratum of society, and among all ages. I want to see the Church being at the forefront and being more effective than it has ever been, in meeting social problems and needs, and in providing solutions based on shared Biblical values and world view. I want God to come to this nation again!

The question I wish to ask is, Do you want the same? For your nation, wherever you live in the world? If God can speak to an ordinary person like me about these things, then He can speak to those who are listening anywhere in the world. If you want to see things change, it is up to you. You can be the channel through which the Spirit of God begins to work, affecting your immediate world of friends, relatives, and colleagues, and then, later, even affecting the nation. Transformation is on God's heart; it always has been.

God wants to use His people to bring change to the nations and communities of the world. He has no "plan B." We are His chosen instruments. How is it going to happen in your nation? Seek God's face. Wait in His presence. Ask Him for a strategy to bring transformation. Meet with others with a similar desire. Compare the words that God has been speaking over and to you and your nation. Move forward in line with what He has said. And pray the words of Jesus:

> Your kingdom come,
> your will be done
>   on earth as it is in heaven.

(Matthew 6:10)

Everything Jesus prayed can and will happen.

For more information
write to the author at:
21 High Beech Close
St Leonards
East Sussex
TN37 7TT
England

Powerful True Stories

Sarah
Sarah Shaw
978-1-85240-511-3 • £8.99 • PB • 176pp

There is Always Enough
Rolland & Heidi Baker
978-185240-287-7 • £8.99 • PB • 192pp

In Rebel Hands
Trish Perkins
978-185240-504-5 • £12.99 • PB • 416pp

Frida
Frida Gashumba
978-185240-475-8 • £8.99 • PB • 176pp

Biblical Teaching

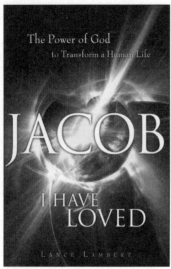

Jacob I Have Loved
Lance Lambert
978-185240-476-5 • £10.99 NOW £9.99 PB • 224pp

Transformed! People – Cities – Nations
Alistair Petrie
978-185240-482-6 • £9.99 • PB • 240pp

Releasing Heaven on Earth
Alistair Petrie
978-185240-481-9 • £9.99 • PB • 272pp

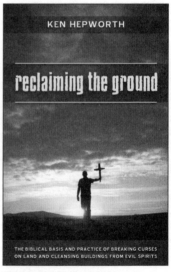

Reclaiming the Ground
Ken Hepworth
978-185240-499-4 • £6.99 • PB • 128pp

Books on Healing

Intercession & Healing
Fiona Horrobin (as featured in the book Sarah)
978-185240-500-7 • £7.99 • PB • 176pp

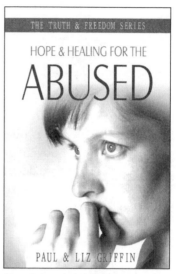

Hope & Healing for the Abused
Paul & Liz Griffin
978-185240-480-2 • £6.99 • PB •128pp

Healing the Past, Releasing your Future
Frank & Catherine Fabiano
978-185240-456-7 • £8.99 • PB • 192pp

Healing through Deliverance (Hardback)
Peter Horrobin
978-185240-498-7 • £19.99 • HB • 586pp

www.sovereignworld.com
View all our titles online or request a catalogue: +44 (0)1524 75 38 05